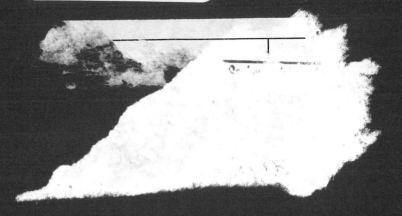

Essential Dog

Essential Dog

The ultimate owner's guide to caring for your dog

Caroline Davis

hamlyn

First published in Great Britain in 2004 by
Hamlyn, a division of Octopus Publishing Group Ltd
2–4 Heron Quays, London E14 4JP

ISBN 0 600 60959 6

A CIP catalogue record for this book is available from the British Library

Printed in Hong Kong

10 9 8 7 6 5 4 3 2 1

The advice given here should not be used as a substitute for that of a veterinary surgeon. No dogs or puppies were harmed in the making of this book.

In this book, unless the information given is specifically for female dogs, dogs are referred to throughout as 'he'. The information is equally applicable to both male and female dogs, unless otherwise specified.

CONTENTS

INTRODUCTION

As I write, there is a dog curled up next to me, a German Shepherd Dog called Hal. Our family has had the pleasure of his company for some 8 years or so now and, for us, Hal represents everything about a dog that owners could wish for. He is gentle and good-natured, playful and obedient, and has his own unique character that we have come to understand and appreciate over the years. As I look at him, all the reasons for owning a dog are clear: quite simply, he is a fantastic pal.

For many people, young and old alike, and particularly those who live alone, their dog is their best friend – and there are many reasons for this. A dog is the ultimate companion. He won't judge our sins, real or imagined, get angry with us, lie to us or cheat us. He may, of course, be miserable if we treat him badly, but he will never blame us – his innocence and trust in us is complete.

It is a well-known fact that dogs are great stress-relievers. Dogs are more willing and receptive to your emotions than humans: who else will happily listen to your moans and groans day in and day out, celebrate with you when no one else is there to share special moments, and comfort you in hours of need.

There are few things more relaxing than getting home from a hard day's work and being welcomed by a creature that is absolutely ecstatic to see you, then taking him for a walk to relieve your mental strains and physical aches.

However, in order to achieve a rewarding and a problem-free relationship with a dog, it is essential to realize that having some inkling of how a dog thinks and feels goes a long way to achieving success in these departments. As with anything in life, the more you put into something, the more you get out of it.

Successful relationships are based on positive two-way communication and respect. By being a fair and positive leader to your dog, you can define a code of practice and behaviour that your dog understands and responds to in the way that you would wish, shaping your new friend into a well-mannered adult that you can be proud of and everyone will admire, love and want to own. Your dog deserves no less.

This book shows that there are many aspects to dog ownership, and there may be topics covered that you have never previously thought about. Prospective owners who read it will see that they must carefully consider all of those elements before taking the plunge and getting a dog, for their own and the animal's sake, while I hope that established owners may well find some information contained within this book invaluable in helping them achieve an even more rewarding and enjoyable relationship with their pet.

CHOOSING A DOG

The question you must ask yourself is: 'I may want a dog, but would a dog want me as his owner?' The decision to have a dog should be a family one. It is not one that can be made lightly and without a great deal of thought. The dog, when you get him, will become an integral part of the family and is likely to remain so for many years. It is important, therefore, that every member of the immediate family should want a dog and be prepared to accept the duties that responsible ownership entails.

Why dogs make good pets

Dogs are traditionally seen as the number one pet. Although the majority are kept as a source of enormous pleasure as a household pet, many dogs still perform the jobs they were originally bred to do. These tasks include herding and guarding duties, as well as being employed as 'eyes and ears' for people with sight and hearing impediments. Dogs are also used to great effect in search-and-rescue situations. All in all, dogs are the most versatile pet humans could wish for. See the checklist for what dogs contribute to our lives.

Checklist

- ✓ affection
- ✓ companionship
- ✓ a sense of security
- ✓ comfort
- ✓ a source of exercise
- ✓ interactive enjoyment
- ✓ a 'listening' ear
- ✓ a way of making new friends

Owning and caring for a dog provides comfort and interest to the lives of people of all ages.

Canine fact

There are now over 300 different breeds of domestic dog recognized by the Kennel Clubs of the UK, the USA, Europe and Australia, from the tiny Chihuahua to the awesome Irish Wolfhound, which stands over 91cm (36in) at the shoulder. All dogs are descended from wolves, which were at one time the most widely distributed mammals in the northern hemisphere.

Companionship

In return for food, shelter and affection, dogs offer unconditional love and loyalty to their owners. Owning a happy, healthy dog is one of the most rewarding pleasures in life, and it gives you opportunities to make new friends while walking your pet and taking him to training classes. Having a dog – as with other pets – also has an advantageous effect in helping people relax and recover from illness, as well as keeping us alert and lively as we age.

Exercise and enjoyment

Walking the dog is not only essential for his well-being, it is also excellent for our health. Just a couple of 20-minute brisk walks help to tone our bodies and maintain cardiovascular fitness. Playing with and training a dog is

Did you know ...?

• Stroking dogs has been proven to have a beneficial effect on the blood pressure of the human doing the stroking. So, as well as being pleasurable for the dog, it is good for you too.

• Dogs can bring comfort and help to those whose mental or emotional condition makes it difficult for them to relate to their fellow human beings.

good fun for both parties. Few things are more entertaining than a session of playing 'fetch' with a ball.

Affection

A dog's love of affection from his owners is what makes him special to us; love and loyalty are high on the list of characteristics owners required in a dog. Naturally social creatures that evolved as pack animals, dogs just live to please their owners, because in return they are provided with everything they need to survive comfortably. Some types of dog are more affectionate than others, so people who require such a dog should read up on the various breeds to ensure they end up with a pet that adores being cuddled and petted, as opposed to one that prefers more restrained affection on its own terms.

Security and independence

There is no doubt that, for those who live on their own, having another living being in the home gives confidence. To ensure that your dog remains healthy means that you have to organize your life to a certain extent to accommodate him, and this in itself helps people to maintain direction and order in their lives.

Dogs are efficient warning systems too – they are quick to alert their owners to anything untoward such as a house fire, and have also been known to save people in other types of danger. It is their acute sense of hearing that has made dogs invaluable in their roles as hearing dogs for the deaf, while their trainability enables dogs to act as guides for visually impaired people as well as act as 'home helps' for the disabled.

Dogs are good for your health: playing with and walking a dog ensures you get plenty of regular exercise.

Canine fact

There is an old saying that goes 'Every child should have a dog and parents who'll let him have one'. Research from Warwick University (published in *Your Dog* magazine in 2002) has shown that children who are brought up with a dog do better at school, are more relaxed and confident, are more responsible and have a healthier respect for their fellow creatures.

Cross-breed or pedigree?

Before getting a dog, you will need to make a number of decisions, including selecting the breed and type of dog you would like. You may have in mind the ideal appearance, colour, type and temperament, but would the type of dog you have in mind fit without any problems into your lifestyle and fulfil your expectations? You will need to consider all the items on the checklist.

Checklist

- ✓ your experience of dogs
- ✓ suitability of the type
- ✓ temperament traits
- ✓ size and age of dog
- ✓ upbringing and early socialization
- ✓ purchase cost
- ✓ longevity and health prospects
- ✓ sex
- ✓ breed characteristics
- ✓ appearance
- ✓ daily care and exercise requirements
- ✓ coat maintenance
- ✓ food requirements
- ✓ cost of holiday care
- ✓ accommodation requirements
- ✓ potential hereditary defects
- ✓ trainability
- ✓ whether it is good with children

Where your living accommodation and exercise facilities are concerned, dog size matters. Choose a pet that will fit comfortably in both; the large Dobermann needs plenty of space, while the tiny Chihuahua will be comfortable anywhere.

Your lifestyle

This determines, to a great extent, what sort of pet you should be looking for. In the dog's lifetime, you are responsible for his health and mental well-being, and must find others to maintain these things if you are unable to, for instance when you are on holiday or have to be away from home.

Some breeds, compared to others, are high-maintenance, so only consider these types if you are able to provide daily care and attention for them for the next 15 years or so. If you get a dog with a coat that necessitates a lot of grooming, or requires clipping on a regular basis, you must be prepared to learn how to care for his coat properly; if you choose an extrovert, energetic type with high exercise needs, then you must have the time to cater for him. Such considerations may seem obvious, but animal welfare organizations still have to cope with thousands of abandoned animals that their owners felt unable to care for.

Ultimately, picking a pedigree or non-pedigree dog is your decision. However, armed with a fair amount of knowledge you are in the best position to make an informed choice and, therefore, end up with a pet that fulfils all your basic requirements.

Top tip

Before making an impulse purchase, do your homework and read up about canine breeds to ensure that you choose the most suitable type possible for your lifestyle. Spend some time, also, learning about canine psychology, as understanding what makes dogs 'tick' results in a much more stress-free and enjoyable relationship between dog and owner.

How you will turn the dog into the companion you desire, given your lifestyle and expectations of him, is detailed in the following chapters.

Personal preference

You may have in mind the ideal dog in colour, type and temperament: one that looks attractive, is affectionate towards you and behaves perfectly in all respects. However, bear in mind that dogs are living beings – each is an individual with his own character make-up. You cannot, therefore, buy one 'off the shelf', programmed to be the perfect pet you envisage.

You can choose your preferred colour and type but, to a great extent, the way the dog behaves and relates to you will depend on how you care for, handle and interact with him. Some pedigree dogs are known for certain character traits, such as a laid-back attitude and a strong affection for humans, and this can make the job of choosing a dog easier if you do your homework.

The options

Dogs are available in three varieties:
• pure-bred (pedigree)
• cross-bred (pedigree parents of different breeds)
• mongrel (a dog with one or both parents cross-breds or mongrels)
Cost may influence your choice, but bear in mind that pure-breds are not necessarily superior to cross-breds or

Dogs bred to herd (the Collie) and hunt (the Spaniel) need lots of exercise and stimulation.

mongrels – indeed in terms of health the reverse is generally true, as many pure-bred dogs are prone to physical and psychological problems caused, initially, by limited gene pools and, later, by a lack of selective breeding.

Frequently asked question

Q I have two young children and we have decided that it would be nice to offer a rescue dog a home. Are there any particular considerations I should be aware of?

A Pedigrees, cross-breeds and mongrels of all ages are available from animal welfare centres, but as you have young children it would be best to avoid getting an adult of any type of unknown origins, as the dog may prove less tolerant than a puppy and could become snappy. Most rescue centres are aware of the difficulties in placing adult dogs, and carefully match them as closely as possible with new owners.

PEDIGREE, CROSS-BREED OR NON-PEDIGREE?

TYPE	PROS	CONS
Pedigree 	• Having researched the breed, you can pinpoint your ideal pet, knowing, usually, what to expect in terms of appearance and character. • There are many specific types and colours to choose from. • Pedigrees are usually raised with the greatest of care, so you should expect a healthy animal.	• Pedigrees are more expensive than cross-breeds. • Some breeds are prone to hereditary problems, or particular ailments. • Some breeds have particular character traits, or care requirements, that may not be appealing, or practical for your lifestyle or requirements. • Certain breeds can be difficult to obtain as they are rare, or the demand for the breed exceeds availability.
Cross-breed 	• Usually less expensive than pedigrees. • Knowing what the parents are like, you have a fair idea of what to expect in terms of appearance and character. • Generally more hardy than pedigrees, but this does depend on the cross and the genetic parentage. • Because the crosses are usually intended, you can normally expect the resulting animals to have been raised with care and therefore be well socialized and healthy; but this is not always the case, so beware.	• Not always easily available – especially if you want a particular cross-breed. • Due to the character/behaviour traits of the breeds involved, certain combinations can be quite 'explosive', resulting in a highly demanding, exhausting or even daunting pet (for example a Border Collie x English Springer Spaniel – although there are always exceptions to every rule).
Non-pedigree 	• Free, or inexpensive. • Wide type and colour choice. • Usually easily available. • Generally few health complications.	• The character traits of the parents are generally unknown, so, to an extent, how the dog will turn out in terms of looks, behaviour and character is uncertain. • You may have to wait a while to find the age, colour and sex of your choice. • You cannot always be sure that the animal has been properly raised and cared for, so beware of any signs of ill health, behaviour problems and character defects.

Did you know ...?

Dogs come in all shapes and sizes to suit all requirements and tastes. However, some breeds' actual physical appearances are altered by humans to display a certain look; the main methods used are tail docking and ear cropping (which should only be carried out by a veterinary surgeon), although various countries have different views and laws regarding both types of mutilation (as these are subject to change, always check the latest legislation in the relevant country), and an increasing number of dogs are now being left as nature intended. Examples of both ear cropping and tail docking include the Dobermann, ear cropping is seen on the Great Dane, and tail docking is seen in the Rottweiler. Some breeds have exaggerated features bred in, such as squashed-in faces (technically called brachycephalic), but where there is any great deviation from normal it is likely that the animal will suffer health problems stemming from these 'abnormalities'.

What's in a name?

Pedigree dog breeds are categorized into named groups to differentiate their particular uses, that is, what they were originally bred to do.

• **Hounds** – comprising 'sight' hounds (which chase their quarry on sighting it) and 'scent' hounds (which source their quarry by its scent). They include Greyhound, Beagle, Basenji and Rhodesian Ridgeback, among many others.

• **Gundogs** – those breeds used to find, flush out and retrieve game, the best known being the Pointers, Retrievers and Spaniels.

BASIC BREED CHARACTERISTICS

GROUP	CHARACTERISTICS
Herding dogs	Responsive to training; very active by nature; extremely sensitive and prone to stereotypic behaviour if their intelligence and energy is not correctly handled; very loyal; need lots of exercise and mental stimulation.
Hounds	Affectionate and friendly, but highly independent and therefore more difficult to train than dogs of other groups.
Gundogs	Popular as companions, as their inbred instinct is to work on an individual basis with their owners; tend to be good-natured, tolerant, keen to please and quick to learn.
Terriers	Lively, curious and tenacious with strong and determined personalities; often 'bossy', quite vocal; may be suspicious of strangers and not always tolerant of children.
Guard and working breeds	Temperament will be influenced by their breeding, upbringing and early environment/socialization; tend to be strong-willed and can be become 'too big for their boots' if not handled appropriately.
Toy breeds	Small in size and generally friendly and affectionate, though can be brave watchdogs.

• **Terriers** – dogs bred to go to ground to kill/flush out vermin. Examples include Bedlington Terrier, Bull Terrier, Australian Terrier, German Hunting Terrier and Parson Jack Russell Terrier.

• **Utility (also known as Non-sporting)** – some may have been bred for a particular task, but now are bred to be companion dogs. Examples include Dalmatian, originally a carriage dog, and Chow Chow, which the Chinese bred for food and fur.

• **Working** – the group encompasses those dogs bred for guarding (in the security field) or for working (hauling, rescue and sled). Examples include Rottweiler, Dobermann, Leonberger, Boxer, Siberian Husky, Pyrenean Mountain Dog, St Bernard, Japanese Akita, Dogue de Bordeaux and Great Dane, among many.

• **Pastoral (also known as herding)** – includes dogs bred to herd cattle, sheep and other livestock. Included in this group, among many, are German Shepherd Dog, Collies,

SPECIFIC BREED TRAIT EXAMPLES

BREED	TYPE	TRAITS
Greyhound	Hound (sight)	Large though slender framed. Good-natured and affectionate; likes to have a good gallop, but more than happy to be a 'couch potato'; retired Greyhounds make excellent pets in any size home, although must be carefully socialized with cats and other small pets. Clean and needs minimal grooming.
Rhodesian Ridgeback	Hound (scent)	Large with solid frame. Good-tempered, loyal family dog if correctly socialized as a puppy. Needs proper handling as an adult for him to remain well balanced. Needs lots of exercise; plenty of living space and minimal grooming.
Boxer	Working	Medium-sized and sturdy frame. Needs firm early training and plenty of exercise to become a devoted pet and enthusiastic playmate. Needs plenty of exercise, at least average living space and minimal grooming.
Pyrenean Mountain Dog	Pastoral (herding)	Giant-sized with solid, powerful frame. Gentle and serious; needs careful socializing to ensure a good-tempered and biddable adult dog suitable for all the family. Needs plenty of living space, exercise and a lot of regular grooming.
Weimaraner	Gundog (sporting)	Medium/large-sized with solid frame. Fearless, protective, obedient and friendly. Good all-round family dog, providing correctly raised and socialized, that needs plenty of living space and exercise. Minimal grooming.
Bedlington Terrier	Terrier	Small with slender frame. Quiet, gentle, affectionate and playful with people, but not reliable and even ferocious with other dogs. Needs regular grooming/clipping, but does not shed coat so may be a good choice for allergy sufferers.
Chinese Crested	Toy	Miniature with slender frame. Alert and intelligent watchdogs as well as good companions. Hairless, apart from a flowing crest on the head and tail plume, so minimal grooming and may be ideal for allergy sufferers.

Sheepdog, Newfoundland, Welsh Corgis and Briard.

• **Toy breeds** – small breeds traditionally bred as lap dogs, although many make excellent guards and are very courageous in the face of danger. Examples include Pekingese, Pomeranian, Miniature Pinscher, Affenpinscher, Cavalier King Charles Spaniel, Australian Silky Terrier, and Yorkshire Terrier (even though it was originally bred by Yorkshire weavers in the 1840s to kill rats).

The right dog for you

Pedigree dogs are not necessarily more loving, clever or naughty than other dogs, and each breed's appearance is a matter of taste. Working dogs tend to be more demanding of their owners,

companion dogs tend to be more laid-back and cross-breeds tend to be generally thought of as being 'hardy'. Whatever the type or breeding, an animal's character is also determined by the way it is reared and its handling by humans. Whether you get a pedigree or non-pedigree dog, the costs of neutering, vaccinating, feeding and caring for him will be just the same. The only difference will be in the initial cost of acquiring him.

The flow charts on the following pages are intended as at-a-glance guide examples to finding the right sort of dog to suit different lifestyles – theirs and yours – for a fulfilling and happy relationship.

Canine fact

A discovery in 1928 of the so-called Windmill Hill dog in excavations at a Neolithic settlement near Avebury in Wiltshire, England, showed that the process of domestication and selective breeding of dogs in Britain, as elsewhere in Europe, was already under way 5,000 years ago. Babylonian (now Iraqi) art of the same period depicted huge Mastiff-like dogs of massive frame which were probably used as guards or in war. These were in sharp contrast to the smaller and more slender Windmill Hill dog, and the hunting dogs bred by the Assyrians some 2,000 years later.

Frequently asked question

Q Although I would like to have a dog, I am allergic to them. Is there any breed or type that would not cause me to have a reaction?

A Recent research in America has shown that dogs are worse for asthma sufferers than cats. It is the allergen Fel d1 present in cat saliva and secreted from sebaceous glands in cats that causes a problem, while in dogs the allergen Can d1 (from the saliva and urine) is the culprit, along with microscopic dander (skin flakes) from both animals. Some people with allergies report that certain breeds of dog are easier to live with than others, for example those whose coats do not shed (such as the Poodle and Bichon Frisé) and those who are virtually coatless (such as hairless dogs). However, the dogs need to be kept clean to keep allergens on the coat and skin to a minimum. There are products available that remove those allergens from the coat and prevent them getting into the air; these, along with regular vacuuming and dusting, can prove helpful in alleviating allergy symptoms. Nevertheless, some people are so severely affected that any contact with pets results in a serious allergy attack.

Poodles are often chosen as pets by those who are normally allergic to canines, as this breed does not shed hair and lacks the distinctive 'doggy' smell.

What type of dog will suit your lifestyle?

Longhaired breeds need correct grooming on a daily basis to remain matt-free, healthy and looking good.

Young active couple; large house; remote rural area; lots of off-lead exercise opportunity →	**Experienced owners; require security/ watchdog and companionship** →	**Hair and slobber OK** → Briard, Rough Collie, German Shepherd Dog, Newfoundland, St Bernard, Leonberger, Afghan Hound, Borzoi, Scottish Deerhound
		Medium to giant dog preferred
		Prefer easy-care coat → Rhodesian Ridgeback, Great Dane, Rottweiler, Lurcher, Bloodhound, Shorthaired German Shepherd Dog, English Springer Spaniel, Irish Wolfhound, Setters and Pointers, Dobermann, Bullmastiff

Active person; small house and garden; built-up residential area; off-lead exercise necessitates car →	**Experienced owner; requires active, happy pet for exercise and companionship** →	**Requires easy-care smooth coat** → Whippet, Lancashire Heeler, Jack Russell Terrier, Chihuahua, Shorthaired Dachshund, Boston Terrier
		Small dog preferred
		No objection to grooming → Miniature/Toy Poodle, Cavalier/King Charles Spaniel, Pomeranian, Yorkshire Terrier, Maltese, Affenpinscher, West Highland White Terrier, American/English Cocker Spaniel, Dandie Dinmont Terrier, Border Terrier, Bedlington Terrier

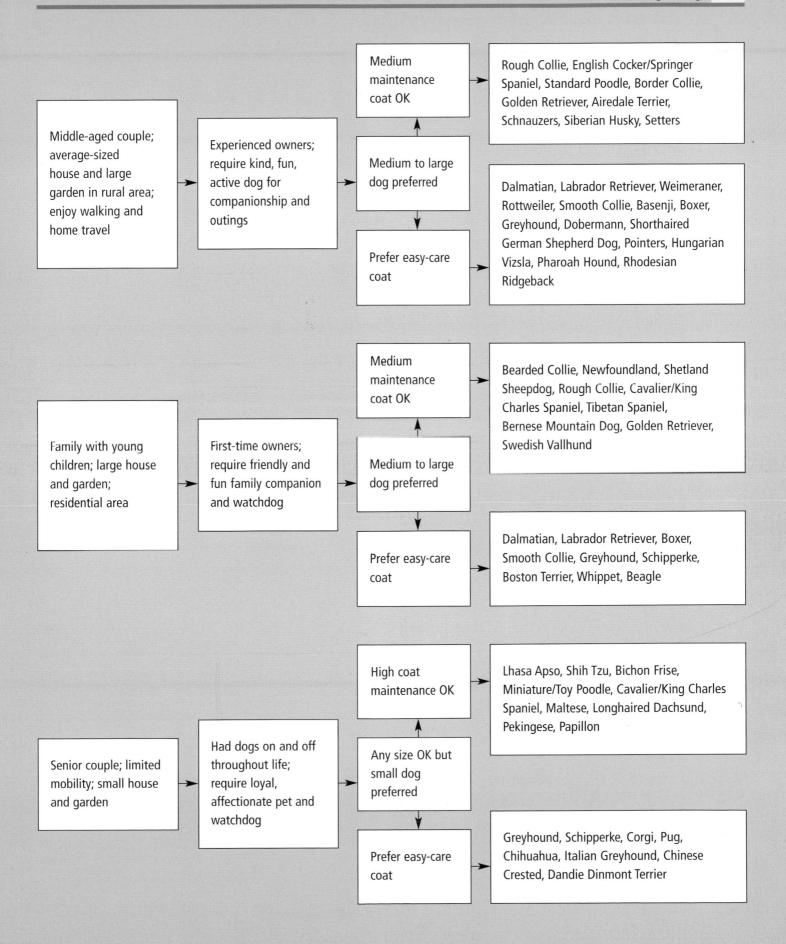

Middle-aged couple; average-sized house and large garden in rural area; enjoy walking and home travel → **Experienced owners; require kind, fun, active dog for companionship and outings** →

Medium maintenance coat OK → Rough Collie, English Cocker/Springer Spaniel, Standard Poodle, Border Collie, Golden Retriever, Airedale Terrier, Schnauzers, Siberian Husky, Setters

Medium to large dog preferred

Prefer easy-care coat → Dalmatian, Labrador Retriever, Weimeraner, Rottweiler, Smooth Collie, Basenji, Boxer, Greyhound, Dobermann, Shorthaired German Shepherd Dog, Pointers, Hungarian Vizsla, Pharoah Hound, Rhodesian Ridgeback

Family with young children; large house and garden; residential area → **First-time owners; require friendly and fun family companion and watchdog** →

Medium maintenance coat OK → Bearded Collie, Newfoundland, Shetland Sheepdog, Rough Collie, Cavalier/King Charles Spaniel, Tibetan Spaniel, Bernese Mountain Dog, Golden Retriever, Swedish Vallhund

Medium to large dog preferred

Prefer easy-care coat → Dalmatian, Labrador Retriever, Boxer, Smooth Collie, Greyhound, Schipperke, Boston Terrier, Whippet, Beagle

Senior couple; limited mobility; small house and garden → **Had dogs on and off throughout life; require loyal, affectionate pet and watchdog** →

High coat maintenance OK → Lhasa Apso, Shih Tzu, Bichon Frise, Miniature/Toy Poodle, Cavalier/King Charles Spaniel, Maltese, Longhaired Dachsund, Pekingese, Papillon

Any size OK but small dog preferred

Prefer easy-care coat → Greyhound, Schipperke, Corgi, Pug, Chihuahua, Italian Greyhound, Chinese Crested, Dandie Dinmont Terrier

Puppy or adult?

Many people only think of getting a puppy, but that may not be the best choice for their circumstances or lifestyle; the character of an older dog is easier to see and any difficult or undesirable traits will already be apparent. Consider all the points on the checklist before you decide.

Checklist
- ✓ your lifestyle
- ✓ your circumstances
- ✓ your time available
- ✓ your requirements
- ✓ your other pets (if applicable)
- ✓ the age practicalities (human and animal)

PUPPY OR ADULT: AT-A-GLANCE GUIDE

AGE	PROS	CONS
Puppy	• Puppies and young adults tend to be more adaptable than their mature counterparts, but it really does depend on many circumstances and characters. • You can enjoy seeing a puppy grow and develop. • You will, hopefully, have many years to enjoy together. • To a great extent, it will be easier to train him to behave in the way you require.	• A young puppy needs small feeds at regular intervals during the day at first, opportunities to go outside to relieve himself after meals, and plenty of attention in order to shape desirable behaviour and properly socialize him, all of which are time-consuming. • A puppy may find it frightening to be introduced into a busy family unless he has been brought up in such an environment and been well socialized with humans (and possibly other pets) since birth. • If there are young children in the house, they will need a good deal of supervision while around and handling the puppy to ensure he is not inadvertently hurt or tormented. • He will not have been neutered.
Adult	• Not as time-consuming as a puppy. • He is likely to have been house-trained. • Character established. • Potentially socialized with people and other animals. • He may have been obedience-trained. • Potentially neutered.	• Limited lifespan depending on age. • He may take longer to bond with you and other pets. • A puppy may be more difficult to integrate into your family. • He may be carrying a disease or ailment. • He may have undesirable behaviour traits that only become apparent when he has settled into your home.

If you already have a dog, ensure that a new pet does not prefer to spend more time with your dog than with you.

Top tip

For the safety of both parties, never allow children to chase after or grab at a puppy or an adult dog.

Dogs and children

Very young children cannot be expected to know how to approach and handle a dog correctly, so it is imperative that they are supervised at all times when together to prevent accidents. Naturally, children want to explore their new pet and play with him, but poking him in the ear or disturbing him when he is eating or sleeping is certainly not the best way to do this.

If your children are taught how to handle dogs with gentleness and respect, then most children and dogs become the best of friends. See pages 88–89 for more detailed information on this subject.

Which sex?

If your dog or puppy is to be neutered, then the question of its sex becomes less important as there will be little difference between males and females. How loving and obedient the dog will be depends on how he is brought up and treated by his owner. See pages 144–147 for detailed information on neutering.

One dog or two?

Is it a good idea to get another dog as a companion for your existing one? Having two dogs can work very well for all concerned, but it can also have drawbacks if you do not take care to make sure that they do not bond closer to each other than to you, or you may end up with problems in training them and in their learning undesirable traits from each other. See pages 82–83 for more detailed information on this subject.

Did you know ...?

Bear in mind that if you choose a young mongrel of unknown origins, he may grow unexpectedly large, whereas the adult size of a pedigree dog is fairly standard and predictable. Most puppies are a similar size at birth, but large feet tend to suggest that a mongrel pup will grow into a relatively large dog.

When to get a dog

You may want a dog, but stop and think – would a dog want to be with you right at this moment in your life? Wanting a dog and actually getting one are two very different things. Whether you choose an adult dog or a puppy, you must take into account your personal circumstances at the relevant time. There are many things to consider – see the checklist – before welcoming a dog into your home.

Checklist

✓ availability of puppies or adult dogs
✓ booked holidays
✓ work commitments
✓ stressful times
✓ pregnancy
✓ time of year
✓ family commitments
✓ personal circumstances

Get the timing right

Are you ready to get a dog? The time may not ideal to get one if you are:
• moving house
• hectically busy at work and socially
• changing jobs

Make sure that the time to get a dog is right for all the family.

• being made redundant
• in the throes of an illness
• separating from your partner
• mourning a death in the family
• expecting a new baby
• due to go on holiday
• faced with losing your job
• about to celebrate a momentous occasion that will result in family routine upheaval and an increase in household activity or noise levels

There are always exceptions to the rules, and many people find comfort in their pets at times when they are suffering great stress. Such owners may feel that, although they are in turmoil, their pets are not suffering in any way because they remain fed and cared for. However, it is a known fact that animals do feel their owners' anxieties (this is called anxiety transference) and feel worried themselves. These anxieties may manifest in unusual behaviour such as attention-seeking or soiling around the home.

It is important, therefore, to ensure that you are in a position both materially and emotionally to offer a secure and harmonious home to a dog before you get one.

Holidays

Wait until you have been on vacation before getting a dog, because otherwise he will suffer upheaval twice in a very short space of time – initially when you remove him from his former home, and then when you disappear and either leave him in a boarding kennels or with a trusted carer. For him to remain mentally and physically well, a new pet needs a good

Dogs, especially puppies, are adorable and it is easy to get one on impulse – but restrain yourself and seriously consider if the time is really right to get a canine friend.

deal of time to settle in and feel secure in his new home before anything out of the ordinary occurs, such as being displaced from that home – even for a short while.

Dog availability

Sometimes it may not be as easy to get a dog as you may imagine. There are several reasons for this:
• If you desire a particular breed, colour or sex of puppy or adult, it may not be available 'on spec'; you may have to reserve a specific requirement with a breeder (or even several breeders) so that when such an animal becomes available you have first choice.
• Puppy availability depends on breeding seasons.
• There may not immediately be the exact type of dog you want at rescue centres, so you may have to be prepared to wait some time.
• Puppies tend to be in high demand at rescue centres, so you may to wait until one becomes available.

Frequently asked question

Q I want to get a dog but I am expecting a baby. Is it best to get a dog before or after the birth?

A This is debatable, but it is probably better to wait until you have the baby before introducing a new dog. He will then view the infant as one of the family, rather than an unwelcome intrusion into their life. If you have pets, toxoplasmosis and toxocariasis (see page 89) are of concern to new mothers but, providing you worm your pets correctly and adhere to household hygiene rules, this risk should be minimal.

Where to get a dog

There are many avenues to investigate when searching for a dog – from pedigree dog breeders and owners of a mongrel that has produced puppies to an animal rescue centre. The decision is yours, but it helps to be fully informed of all possible advantages and disadvantages before you make it. Potential sources are given in the checklist.

Checklist

✓ breeders
✓ private homes
✓ rescue centres
✓ finding a stray
✓ pet stores
✓ friends and family

Did you know ...?

Puppies are not always available throughout the year; fewer are born in the late winter than during the spring and summer months.

Finding a dog

Your local paper, pet stores, vet surgery notice boards, dog magazines, word of mouth through friends and family and rescue centres are all potential sources of finding an adult dog or puppy. If you want a puppy, bear in mind that he should be at least 6 weeks old before he can safely leave his mother. By this time, he should be fully weaned on to puppy

When buying from a breeder, insist on seeing both parents, or at least the mother, so that you can get a good idea of looks and temperament. Litters brought up inside the house as part of the family will be better socialized as pet dogs than those kept outside.

Top tip

Some dogs are naturally quiet and staid in their habits, while others are extroverted clowns. It is possible that you will see both types in the same litter. A noisy, busy household with young children and other pets is not the place for a timid and sensitive adult dog or puppy, and an exuberant, mischievous canine might prove a little too lively for a quiet and peaceful home.

food and ideally be socialized with a wide range of people and other animals. Some breeders prefer to wait until their puppies are older before homing, so that they are fully house-trained and have had their initial vaccinations.

Which source is best?

There are considerations to take into account with all of them, as described below, and no one source is best.

Dog breeders

When choosing a puppy, whether pedigree or not, it is always best to select him from a whole litter if possible. The appearance of the young puppies will influence your choice,

but so too should their behaviour and health; it is preferable to pick one that appears healthy (see page 28), outgoing, frisky and friendly and approaches you confidently. Don't pick an animal that looks unhealthy (see page 29) or you may just be taking on a problem; look elsewhere instead.

Sometimes it is possible to get an older pedigree dog from a breeder who has no further use for that particular one, or puppies resulting from accidental matings or not suited to a breeding programme. Breeders sometimes insist that such dogs are neutered so they cannot be bred from.

Friends and family

Opting for an older, house- and obedience-trained dog can be a good idea if you do not have the time to spend training a puppy, particularly if you are offered a well-behaved animal by a friend.

Rescue centres or animal welfare shelters

If you decide to choose a pet from an animal shelter or rescue centre, find out as much as you can from the staff about his background. Some dogs, for example, will not be house-trained if they were formerly strays.

Strays

Sometimes a dog simply moves into a home where he finds a welcome, or you may come across one that you think has

HOW MUCH WILL A DOG COST?

SOURCE	COST
Pedigree breeder	Depending on the breed and whether or not the dog is of show quality, prices range enormously, so it pays to shop around.
Friends and family	Non-pedigree puppies or adults are generally free 'to good homes'; part-pedigree and pedigrees can vary in cost depending on the reason for re-homing.
Rescue centre	There is generally a charge to cover the cost of neutering and vaccinations.
Strays	Free.
Pet store	Prices vary: pedigree dogs are more expensive than non-pedigree.

Staff at a good rescue centre will be able to give you accurate information about the dog you are interested in, and help you make the right choice.

been abandoned. However, if you do find a 'stray', be aware that someone somewhere could be grieving over the disappearance of their pet, so make every effort to trace his owners by informing the local authorities, local animal welfare shelters, putting up 'found' posters in local stores and veterinary surgeries, and by having the animal checked for a microchip at the vet's. Once you have satisfied yourself that he is indeed a stray, have him checked over by a vet to ensure he is healthy, and also have him neutered if necessary.

Pet stores or 'puppy farms' (multibreed kennels)

Ensure that the animals look well cared for, have adequate space, food and water and appear healthy. If many dogs are kept together in a less-than-ideal environment, and there is a constant turnover of 'stock', there is a high risk of infection being present, which may not manifest itself until you get your new pet home. Buying a dog from a pet store or 'puppy farm' is not recommended.

Canine fact

If you pick a dog from a rescue centre, then, as well as finding yourself a pet, you will have the pleasure of knowing that you have probably saved a life since many unwanted animals have to be destroyed. Elderly dogs are more difficult to re-home than their younger counterparts so, if you require a quiet, laid-back pet, then do consider a 'golden oldie'. Older dogs will live for fewer years, which may be an advantage if you are elderly yourself. In addition, they are more likely to tolerate being left alone while you go to work, and will, with luck, have a track record of living successfully as a pet dog.

Frequently asked question

Q We would like a pedigree dog but are unsure as to what all the breeds are, and which one would be best. Without travelling all over the country to see different breeders, how can we learn what the different breeds are and what they look like?

A It is a good idea to visit a championship dog show, where you will see many different ages, breeds and colours all under one roof. You can see what a particular breed of dog will mature into, and you may have the chance to glean information from breeders and owners about the types you are particularly drawn to. You will find shows advertised in dog magazines and by breed/canine societies on the internet. If travelling to a show is not possible, then obtain a good book on dog breeds. Having decided which breed you like, the next step is to contact the governing body of pedigree breeds (which are also, generally, to be found in dog magazines) in order to get details of breeders of that type of dog.

Depending on the country, dog shows are held on a regular basis and can be one- or two-day events. Entry to shows as spectators is not expensive, and breeders who are exhibiting are normally listed in the show catalogue.

Signs to look for in a healthy dog

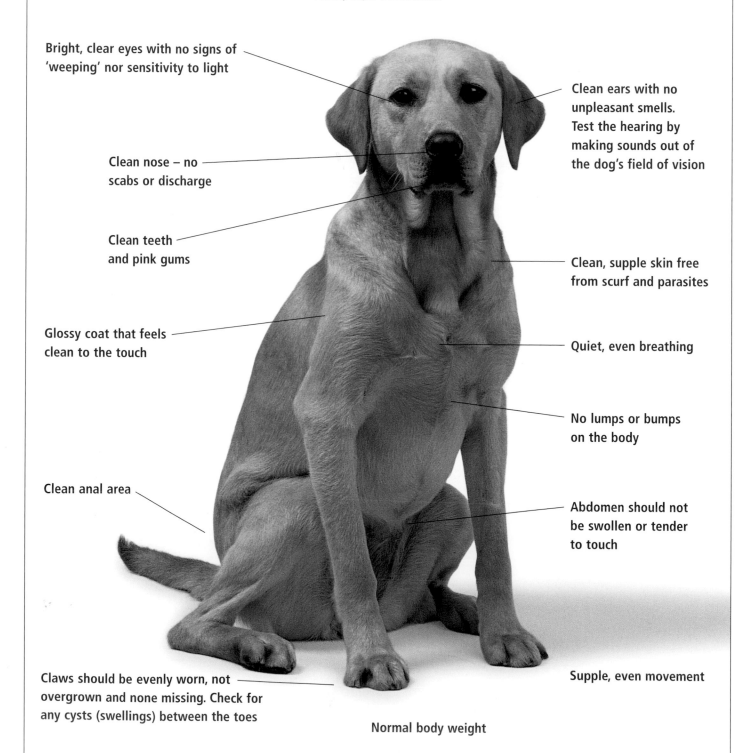

Alert, calm demeanour

Bright, clear eyes with no signs of 'weeping' nor sensitivity to light

Clean ears with no unpleasant smells. Test the hearing by making sounds out of the dog's field of vision

Clean nose – no scabs or discharge

Clean teeth and pink gums

Clean, supple skin free from scurf and parasites

Glossy coat that feels clean to the touch

Quiet, even breathing

No lumps or bumps on the body

Clean anal area

Abdomen should not be swollen or tender to touch

Claws should be evenly worn, not overgrown and none missing. Check for any cysts (swellings) between the toes

Supple, even movement

Normal body weight

Signs to look for in an unhealthy dog

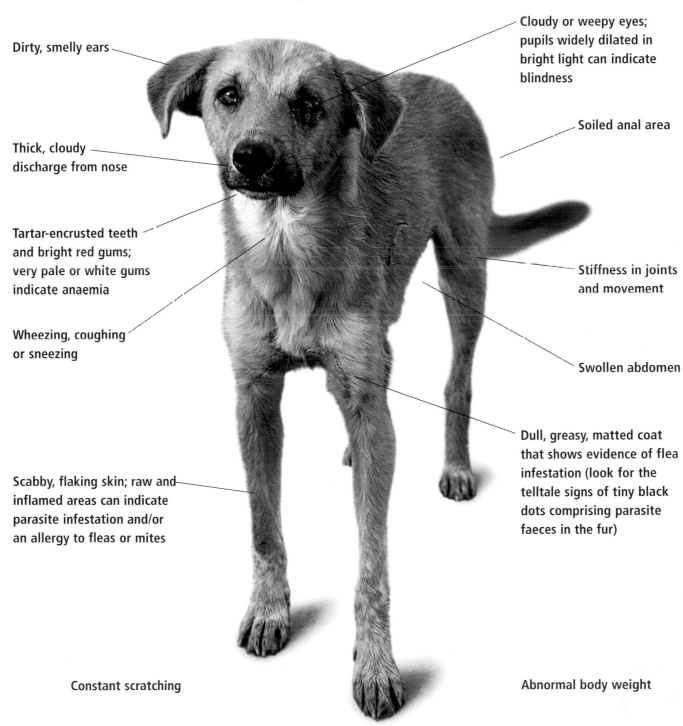

Depressed demeanour

Cloudy or weepy eyes; pupils widely dilated in bright light can indicate blindness

Dirty, smelly ears

Soiled anal area

Thick, cloudy discharge from nose

Tartar-encrusted teeth and bright red gums; very pale or white gums indicate anaemia

Stiffness in joints and movement

Wheezing, coughing or sneezing

Swollen abdomen

Dull, greasy, matted coat that shows evidence of flea infestation (look for the telltale signs of tiny black dots comprising parasite faeces in the fur)

Scabby, flaking skin; raw and inflamed areas can indicate parasite infestation and/or an allergy to fleas or mites

Constant scratching

Abnormal body weight

Essential equipment

On the market there is a huge, bewildering range of equipment and products designed specially for dogs – many described as something your pet just can't live without. Many of these items are simply not essential, however. You won't need a great deal of equipment to care for your new adult dog or puppy, and what you actually do need tends not to be very expensive. The basic things you will need are given in the checklist, and you can add to these later as you wish or require.

Checklist

- ✔ food and water bowls
- ✔ bed and bedding
- ✔ toys
- ✔ first-aid kit (see page 157)
- ✔ collar with identity tag
- ✔ leash
- ✔ travelling harness or crate
- ✔ grooming gear
- ✔ poop scoop
- ✔ indoor crate
- ✔ an outdoor kennel and pen (if you have room)

Food and water bowls

Your dog should have his own food and water bowls, which cannot be tipped over. Glazed ceramic or stainless steel bowls are the best as they can be cleaned most hygienically and cannot be chewed, but plastic will do. Put the bowls on a wipe-down feeding mat or sheet of newspaper to catch any spills.

Poop scoops

Poop scoops are designed to pick up your dog's faeces easily and hygienically so that you can dispose of the waste, both at home and out on walks, appropriately. Dispose of faeces, well wrapped up in newspaper or biodegradable bags, with your own household rubbish, not down the toilet as this could cause a blockage. When out on walks, carry a small biodegradable plastic bag to put the faeces in and either take it home to dispose of, or place it in a dog waste bin designed for the purpose.

Consult your vet or local waste disposal company as regards disposing of waste from a dog receiving radiation treatment.

Bed and bedding

Choose a bed that will be big enough for the dog when he is fully grown, with raised sides to protect against draughts, and made of easily washed material (see chart opposite). Bedding should be thick enough for him to lie on comfortably, and of an easy-wash, quick-dry material. Blankets, fleece material, old duvets, a cushion/old pillow, and fleecy

Food and water bowls should be large enough to accommodate your size of dog. Special bowls can be bought for dogs with long ears, such as Spaniels, to prevent the ears dangling in food and water, while stands are available to lift bowls off the ground for dogs that find eating at ground level difficult.

BEDS AND BEDDING: AT-A-GLANCE GUIDE

BED TYPE	PROS	CONS
Cardboard box	• Cheap • Readily available • High sides keep out draughts	• Needs replacing regularly • Needs extra bedding • Easily chewed
Plastic	• Inexpensive • Hygienic • Easy to clean • High-sided types keep out draughts	• Needs extra bedding • Easily chewed
Wicker	• Looks attractive	• Expensive • Draughty • Harbours dust and fur; difficult to clean • Needs extra bedding • Easily chewed
Cushioned or fake-fur bed	• Comfortable • No extra bedding usually needed	• Can harbour fleas if not washed regularly • Can be difficult to wash and dry • Expensive • Easily chewed
Bean bags	• Comfortable • Warm • Dogs love them	• Can be time-consuming to remove the polystyrene beads in order to wash the cover • If the beads escape they can take hours to clear up • Easily chewed

Buy a bed that will be large enough for the dog to lie down in comfortably when he is mature; high sides will prevent draughts and thick bedding will provide warmth and protection from pressure sores.

Many dogs adore playing with balls, but it is essential to choose ones bigger than your dog's mouth to minimize the potential for them to become lodged in the throat.

Top tip

A stair gate is vital for keeping a dog out of certain areas in the house, yet because he can still see his family he won't feel isolated.

veterinary pet bedding all make good, insulating bedding material for dogs. Materials should be washed regularly to remove dirt and help to prevent flea infestation.

Toys

Not only is it entertaining for us to play with our dogs, but for them it fulfils their instincts to scent trail, watch, stalk, chase, grab, bite, shake, kill and consume – all of which can be seen at different times in our own docile pets. Moving toys in ways that mimic prey behaviour will result in more fun for your dog and more interest for you.

Throwing toys will entice most dogs to play, as it alerts their chase-catch instinct, and you can use this

instinct to help train your dog to retrieve and recall. Hiding toys for them to sniff out and grab satisfies their scent trail-stalk and catch-kill instincts. Shaking a toy is their way of stunning the 'prey' or causing fatal injuries, making it less likely to fight back. Chewing a toy, or ripping it to shreds (which many dogs do), satisfies their instincts to 'open up the carcass' and rip off chunks of flesh.

Activity toys, along with chews, will keep your dog occupied as required. Activity toys are designed to have biscuits put inside them; your dog will puzzle over getting them out, keeping him busy for ages. Chews must be suitably sized for the dog and must only be given under supervision, because of the risk of choking.

There is a huge variety of toys on the market, specially designed for dogs. Balls on ropes that can be spun in a circle and released, or toys that come with a device that propels them further than humans can throw, provide longer chases that will be appreciated by very active dogs.

Having the right equipment makes owning a dog easier.

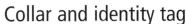

Collar and identity tag

Collars come in many designs, but the most suitable are the broad leather or fabric collar or the half-check (check-choke), which is three-quarters nylon or leather and a quarter chain link. Half-checks are preferred when training, because you can achieve a rattle with the chain part to attract the dog's attention, but because the rest of it is fabric it will not cause damage to the neck.

Your dog should wear a collar complete with an identity tag with his name and telephone number inscribed on it. This is so that he can be identified if he goes missing or is involved in an accident.

When fitting a collar, make sure you can slide two fingers between it and the dog's neck. Check the collar regularly for signs of chafing, and also to see that it still fits comfortably on a growing dog.

Leash

Leashes, like collars, are available in all sorts of lengths and designs, but it is important to choose the most appropriate one for you and your dog. It makes an enormous difference for both parties in terms of comfort and control if you have a leash that is the correct length for the size of your dog, and the right width for your hand.

The leash must be of suitable length to maintain a slack tension. If

There's a wide choice of collars and leashes available, but for ease and effectiveness of handling and training make sure that you choose the right ones.

Top tip

It is *not* a good idea to use a retractable lead when walking your dog near traffic or livestock, as you may not be able to retract the lead the instant it is necessary, which could result in an accident. The retractable mechanism can also wear out through use, or become damaged through getting dirty and/or wet, so check it regularly; you do not want the lead to fail when you need it most.

it is too short, the dog will be dragged along; too long and you will have metres of lead to deal with. Choose a fabric or leather lead that can be extended or shortened as desired (as favoured by dog trainers), and then you will have the best of both worlds when training and when simply out for a walk.

Retractable leashes are available in a variety of designs, but as some are better than others it is imperative that you choose one you can retract easily and instantly when desired. You must also buy the variety suited to the weight of your dog, otherwise it may not be strong enough to control him

(some have been reported to snap when under stress and flick back into the handler's body or face, resulting in serious injury). To be on the safe side, do not use these leads on dogs that pull or become very excitable.

Warning

Choke chains are not advisable, as they are too easy to use inappropriately and cause discomfort or even damage to your dog.

Crate

Also called a den or a cage, a crate serves as a bed and is useful for toilet training, for keeping the dog separate from the family and other pets when necessary, and for safety when travelling with your dog. Crates come in all sizes, with different types of opening. Good, sturdy ones are expensive, so choose one that will be big enough to accommodate your dog when it is fully grown. Cheap crates tend to be badly made and/or flimsy, and therefore represent poor economy because they do not last.

Plastic-covered metal crates are quieter and easier to clean than those

Frequently asked question

Q Is it necessary to have an indoor crate for my dog?

A Although not absolutely essential, an indoor crate (also called a den or a cage) can prove extremely useful. It provides a secure den during a dog's integration period in a new home, and makes the introduction of him to existing pets more manageable and less traumatic. When you cannot be around to supervise young puppies, popping them in the crate will keep them safely away from wires and other hazards that could cause them harm. A crate is also useful when travelling your dog, to keep him and other occupants in the vehicle safe, and it makes a portable temporary kennel when staying with friends or if you take your dog with you on vacation.

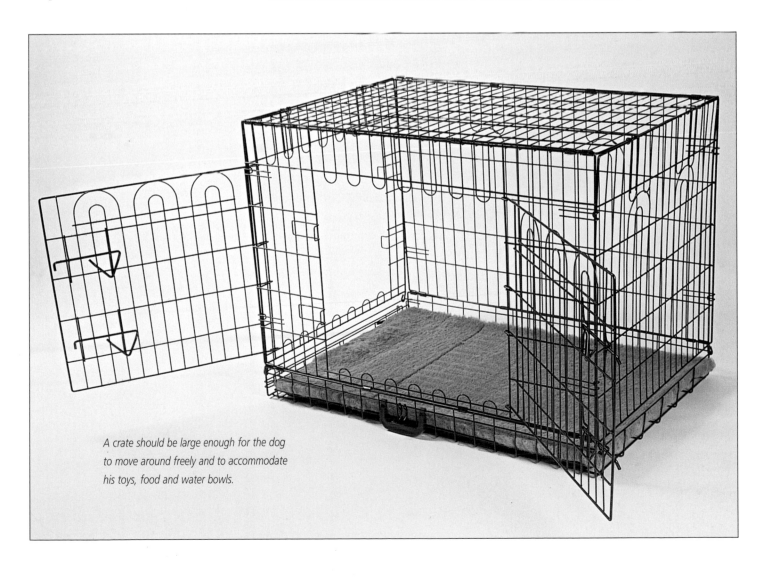

A crate should be large enough for the dog to move around freely and to accommodate his toys, food and water bowls.

Your choice of grooming tools will be influenced by your dog's coat type. A flea comb (right) will help remove fleas from the coat; a slicker brush (centre) is good at removing dead hair; and a wide-toothed comb (left) helps de-mat tangles in long coats.

Top tip

Don't use a flea collar *and* other flea treatments or you may overdose your pet on the chemicals they contain, making him ill.

Get your puppy used to being groomed on a table (put a non-slip mat on it first) if he will need to be professionally groomed later on.

constructed out of bare or galvanized metal. A two-door foldaway crate is more convenient, especially when being used in a vehicle.

Grooming gear

All dogs should be groomed regularly, and some breeds need to be groomed more often than others, in order to keep the coat and skin in good condition, to maintain appearance, to minimize shedding of hair around the home and to prevent matting.

For short-coated breeds, a stiff brush is best. For a medium-length coat, a stiff brush and a hound glove (a silky glove used to give a gloss to the coat) are ideal. To deal with tangles in a long coat, a metal comb is essential. Your dog's breeder and/or local canine beauty salon will advise on the best tools for the job in your dog's particular case.

Owners of breeds that require regular clipping, stripping or trimming sometimes need to invest in the tools needed to do this at home, rather than visiting a professional dog groomer every few weeks. This can be an economical option if you simply want to keep your pet's coat at a suitable length rather than having it styled. However 'professional grooming' is harder than it looks; there is a certain knack to it, so you will have to be shown how to do it in order to get a decent-looking result.

Parasite treatments

Parasites, both internal and external, have a detrimental effect on your dog's health. You will need to treat your dog for internal (worms) and external (fleas, mites and ticks) parasites on a regular basis. The most efficient treatments are only available on prescription from vets, and it is worth spending a little bit more on these as they work efficiently, unlike many shop-bought products. See page 142 for detailed information on this subject.

Kennel and run

A kennel or run can be a useful option for several reasons:

• if your dog is a habitual escape artist when in the garden

• to allow the dog to dry off after a wet, muddy walk

• to control your dog when you have visitors who are afraid of dogs, or don't like them

• to control your dog when visitors bring their own dog(s), and your dog doesn't get on with them

• to let your dog have somewhere to rest in peace when necessary

Having your dog loose in the car is a hazard to the driver, the passengers and the dog. When travelling with your dog, make sure that he is safely secured by means of a harness, crate or dog grille.

Canine first-aid kit

This is essential both for treating minor injuries and for administering emergency first-aid until a vet takes over. You can purchase ready-assembled first-aid kits from pet stores, or from your vet. See page 157 for detailed information on the contents of first-aid kits.

Canine fact

It is possible to train a dog to use an in/out hinged flap set into the door or wall (like a cat flap). This can prove extremely useful to allow your dog free access to a securely fenced garden or yard when he feels like it, or to relieve himself, without you having to be on hand to open the door for him.

Feeding your dog

To maintain your dog's good health, it is essential to feed him a well-balanced diet, and the right amount of it on a daily basis. There is a wide range of canine foods available, so it can be difficult deciding which variety or make is the best choice for your dog. There are, however, certain dietary nutrients that a dog cannot do without (see the checklist), as well as age, health and lifestyle considerations to take into account, and this makes the job of deciding on the most suitable diet much easier.

Checklist

✔ protein
✔ carbohydrates
✔ fat
✔ vitamins
✔ minerals
✔ fibre
✔ water

Eating habits

Dogs are omnivorous in their feeding habits and can be kept satisfactorily on specially formulated vegetarian diets, although they do prefer meat-based foods. In a wild state the dog hunts, kills, feeds, then rests. He may gorge himself on a whole animal one day, then go without food for the next two or three; this is why many dogs are so keen to eat until they are fit to burst – instinct tells them they may have to wait quite a while before their next meal.

Adult domestic dogs are usually fed once a day, but splitting that feed into two meals adds interaction and interest. It is also better to feed certain deep-chested breeds (such as German Shepherd Dogs, Great Danes and Setters) several small meals rather than one big one, to avoid potentially fatal digestive ailments such as bloat (gastric dilation and volvulus).

There are commercially produced clinical diets available, usually only obtainable from vets, which can help dogs suffering from a wide range of diseases, such as kidney stones, signs of senility, obesity, digestive disturbances, diabetes mellitus and tooth and gum problems. There are even foods specifically designed for long-coated breeds, as well as life-stage formulas. You can also choose from holistic diets that contain no artificial additives and diets formulated for allergy sufferers.

Necessary nutrients

Generally, dogs are not difficult to feed, and they thrive on a diet not dissimilar to our own, albeit with a little more protein. Nearly all foods of animal origin, cereals, root vegetables and fats are easy for them to digest. The secret of correct feeding is to give a balanced diet that supplies all essential nutrients in the proper proportions to one another for the purpose intended – work, breeding, growth or healthy adulthood. These nutrients are as follows:

Puppies that are correctly fed are more likely to grow into healthy adult dogs.

Carbohydrates

Carbohydrates, in the form of cooked cereal starch or sugar, can supply up to 70 per cent by weight of the dog's food (after deducting any water present) or about two-thirds of the calories. Dog biscuits, pasta and rice are three useful energy foods for dogs, and rice is a useful foodstuff for dogs with an allergy to wheat.

Proteins

Proteins present in meat and plants (though the latter is inferior to the former) help build body tissue, carry out 'repairs' and make hormones. The dry matter of dog food should contain at least 15 per cent protein, of which at least half should come from animal foods (meat and dairy products), or high-quality vegetable protein such as soya.

Minerals

Minerals are sometimes referred to as 'ash' on dog-food labels. The important ones are calcium, phosphorus and sodium chloride (common salt) in a balanced combination. Calcium and phosphorus make up most of the mineral matter of bone and should be supplied at the rate of about 3 per cent calcium/phosphorus in the diet; too much calcium in the diet, especially in large-breed puppies, can lead to skeletal abnormalities, while too much phosphorus (found in high meat and offal diets) can cause eclampsia in lactating bitches.

Other essential minerals for good health, such as zinc and copper, occur naturally in meat, cereals and other ingredients of a balanced diet.

Vitamins

Vitamin A (also called retinol) is essential for growth and vision, while vitamins of the B group are important for the maintenance, in particular, of the central nervous system.

Top tip

A diet high in protein can be damaging to dogs that suffer from liver and kidney problems. The reason for this is that the body cannot store excess protein so it is excreted, a process putting more pressure on already weak organs responsible for this process.

Frequently asked question

Q My dog is extremely active and gets lots of daily exercise. Does he need a high-protein diet to ensure he gets enough energy?

A No – a diet higher in fat or carbohydrate is better for extremely active dogs as these components put less strain on the liver and kidneys than additional protein.

Water is essential for life itself, and your dog should always have access to a fresh, clean supply. Refill the water bowl each day. Scrub it out regularly with clean water (do not use detergents which would taint the bowl), otherwise the bowl will become slimy with saliva.

Vitamin D helps the body produce calcium, essential for healthy bones and teeth, as is phosphorus. Vitamin E (tocopherol) is vital for the stabilization of cell membranes. Since dogs can produce their own vitamin C (ascorbic acid, essential for maintaining healthy connective tissue and skin), this does not need to be included in the diet.

Fat

Fat adds to food palatability, but is actually only necessary as a source of the essential fatty acids (EFAs, also known as polyunsaturates) that are vital in maintaining body health. They work primarily by controlling water loss through the skin. A deficiency in EFAs can result in reproductive, skin, coat and wound healing problems.

Fibre

A lack of fibre (roughage) in the diet can result – especially in elderly, inactive dogs – in constipation and other digestive problems cause by sluggish bowels. Fibre is supplied through the indigestible plant matter in foods such as cooked and raw vegetables and cereals.

Commercially prepared dog foods are available in (left to right) wet, semi-moist and dry varieties. It can be a case of trying each type to find the one your dog thrives on.

Balancing act

It is important that the balance of nutrients fed to a dog is correct, because excesses can cause as many health problems as deficiencies. If your dog receives more calories (the energy value supplied by foods) per day than his body needs, he will get fat. Just as in humans, obesity is responsible for many canine diseases, such as heart problems, joint ailments and a reduction in lung function.

Did you know ...?

Dry complete food that has been stored too long, particularly in warm or humid conditions, will turn rancid and lose its nutritional value. If you are only feeding one or two dogs, buy only enough food to last a week to ensure the food stays fresh.

Food types

Good-quality proprietary food is the easiest to feed. It contains all the necessary nutrients in the correct proportions, including vitamins and minerals, which could be lacking from a home-made diet of fresh or cooked meat and table scraps. There are four forms of commercially prepared food.

1 Wet/moist (canned or pouch)

Canned food has a high water content, is available in a wide range of flavours and is usually the preferred choice of dogs.

2 Semi-moist (pouch)

Often containing vegetable protein, such as soya, this food type contains less water than canned, therefore keeps well in a bowl without drying out and losing texture.

3 Dry complete

As its name suggests, dry complete food contains minimal water and all the nutrients your dog needs. Some types are designed to be moistened with water before feeding, while other types can be fed as they are, in which case your dog will need plenty of water to drink in conjunction with it.

FOOD TYPES: AT-A-GLANCE GUIDE

FOOD TYPE	PROS	CONS
Wet/moist (canned)	• Extremely palatable • Contains all the nutrients a dog needs • Long storage time if unopened	• Bulky to store and heavy to carry • Takes up space in the refrigerator • Fattening • Strong odour • Not good for teeth • Meat/other ingredient source unidentifiable • Contains many artificial additives • Expensive • Spoils quickly • Can cause digestive upsets in some dogs
Semi-moist (pouches/foil trays)	• Palatable • Contains all the nutrients a dog needs • Easier to store than cans	• Fattening • Strong odour • Not good for teeth • Meat/other ingredient source unidentifiable • Very expensive • Spoils quickly • Takes up space in the refrigerator • Contains man-made artificial additives
Dry complete (packs)	• Economical • Low odour • Contains all the nutrients a dog needs • Better for teeth due to abrasive action when fed dry • Lighter to carry than cans • Convenient to feed	• Bulky to store • Goes off if stored too long • Not as palatable as canned/semi-moist • High cereal content can cause problems for gluten-sensitive dogs
Dry complementary (packs)	• Economical • Low odour • Good source of energy • Most are supplemented with vitamins and minerals • Better for teeth due to abrasive action when fed dry • Lighter to carry than cans • Economical	• Time-consuming to mix with protein-giving ingredients • Spoils if stored too long • Bulky to store
Home-made diet (cooked and/or raw meat, table scraps, cereals, dairy products, fruit and vegetables)	• Economical • Uses up waste food from the table, so environmentally friendly • Raw crunchy vegetables, such as carrots, aid dental hygiene and provide a fresh source of nutrients • Chewing raw meat helps clean the gums and teeth • Sourced ingredients	• Some essential nutrients may be lacking • Fattening if too many table scraps are given • Raw meat may harbour parasites or harmful bacteria • Raw meat spoils quickly • Time-consuming sourcing and preparing ingredients • Strong odour when cooking • Bulky to store/refrigerate pre-prepared food

DAILY FEEDING GUIDE

IDEAL WEIGHT OF ADULT DOG	AMOUNT OF FOOD
2kg (5lb)	110g–140g (4oz–5oz)
5kg (10lb)	200g–280g (7oz–10oz)
10kg (25lb)	400g–570g (14oz–1lb 4oz)
20kg (50lb)	680g–900g (1lb 8oz–2lb)
35kg (75lb)	900g–1.1kg (2lb–2lb 8oz)
45kg (100lb)	1.25–1.6kg (2lb 12oz–3lb 8oz)
70kg (150lb)	1.7–2.5kg (3lb 12oz–5lb 8oz)

Top tip

Your vet will advise you on the ideal weight for your dog, and your mission is to make sure he stays at it. The easiest way to weigh your dog is to weigh yourself, then pick up your dog and weigh yourself again; then subtract the first weight from the second to give you your pet's weight.

Coping with fussy eaters

Dogs don't become bored with a consistent diet of palatable, wholesome food, and their digestions benefit from regularity. Fussy eaters are usually created by their owners; a dog won't usually starve himself unless there is a physical reason, so a selective feeder can be cured within a day or two of giving nothing but the regular diet at set times. If the dog does not eat it up within 20 minutes, remove the food and do not give him anything else until the next mealtime. He will soon start eating properly again.

Most dogs are greedy and will eat anything put in front of them, unless they are suffering from a tooth or stomach ailment.

4 Dry complementary

Designed to be fed with canned, cooked or raw meat, this food usually comprises cereal meal or biscuits. Fed alone, it does not fulfil a dog's daily nutritional needs.

How much should I feed to my dog?

This depends on:
• size
• activity level
• age
• individual nature
• temperature of surroundings

Young dogs and those being worked, or which are very active on a daily basis, may need more food (calories) per day than the average pet dog, whereas an old, inactive dog will require less.

Counting the calories

Energy is measured in units of heat called calories. In a healthy dog, the number of calories he requires balances the number of calories that his body uses each day. If this balance is well maintained, the dog stays fit and healthy and his weight remains constant. An underfed dog gradually loses weight and condition as his body draws on the reserves of fat and protein to make up the deficiencies in his diet.

Feeding good quality puppy food (breed specific if necessary, particularly for giant breeds) is the best way of ensuring a puppy's rapidly growing body receives all the nutrients it needs.

The number of calories a dog needs per day depends on his size, life stage, level of activity and individuality. As an example, a small healthy adult dog with two hours of average activity a day requires anything between 125 and 700 calories per day depending on his size; a large dog will require from 1,400 calories per day, depending on size.

Puppies need more calories in relation to their body weight because they are growing rapidly, are more subject to heat loss due to their small size, and their energy requirements are higher. Lactating bitches need some 50–60 per cent more calories than normal, and highly active (working) dogs need at least 40 per cent more calories than normal moderately active requirements (sled dogs taking part in the famous Iditarod race across the frozen Alaskan wilderness need some 8,000 calories per day to fulfil their energy needs!).

Check the label

Manufacturers' guidelines, as printed on food packs, are a good indicator of how much to feed daily, but beware that they usually err on the excessive side. Decrease or increase your dog's daily intake of food depending on his condition.

Home-made food

Many dogs appreciate 'home-made' foods, but basing an entirely balanced diet around these will be very difficult; a vitamin and mineral supplement will almost certainly be required as well – consult your vet for advice. For ease of feeding (particularly for busy owners), it is simpler to stick to proprietary dog food and only give an occasional home-made meal for a treat, or to tempt a dog that is ill and has lost his appetite. In the case of the latter, items such as cooked porridge, boneless meats and fish, and scrambled eggs are often appreciated and easily digested. Always allow cooked foods to cool before serving.

Chewing on good-sized lumps of raw meat and raw meaty bones helps prevent a build-up of plaque and tartar on the teeth, thereby keeping gums healthy. Bones are rich in minerals too.

Some companies make specially prepared canine birthday cakes comprising suitable, healthy ingredients. It won't hurt to spoil your pet once a year!

Top tip

Although many dogs appear to enjoy eating it, chocolate can make them very ill – and even prove fatal – so do not give it to them as a treat. Instead, give them chocolate drops specially formulated for dogs.

Life-stage feeding

Different feeding regimes are appropriate for the various stages in a dog's life (see chart below).

Dietary extras

On a commercially prepared diet, your dog should not need additional food supplements (comprising vitamins, minerals and oils), unless your vet advises otherwise. Overdosing on nutrients can prove detrimental to your pet's health.

LIFE-STAGE FEEDING

Puppies	Puppies usually stop drinking their mothers' milk and go on to solid food proper when they are 5–6 weeks old; gradual weaning starts at 3 weeks. Once fully weaned onto puppy food, they should be kept on this as it contains all the essential nutrients they need in a form that is easy for them to digest and utilize. Fed correctly at this age, they will be on course to grow into healthy and well-developed adults.
From weaning to 20 weeks	Puppies should receive three meals a day, plus an evening dish of milk.
From 20 to 30 weeks	Three meals a day.
From 30 weeks to 9 months	Two meals a day (depending on breed/growth rate).
From 9 months to 8 years	One or two meals a day.
From 8 years onwards (elderly)	One or two meals a day depending on your pet's condition and health.

When should I feed my dog?

Most owners feed either in the morning or the evening, and sometimes both, depending on their dog's age needs or individual preference. Some dogs fare better with their daily ration split into two or even three meals, while others are happy to eat their daily allowance in one helping (providing it is safe for them to do so – see 'Eating habits' on page 38 – and never work a dog on a full stomach).

It is best not to feed adult dogs at the same times every day, because relying on a rigid routine can prove distressing for a dog should you be late home and are not able to feed at the expected time. Not knowing when it will be fed also helps keep a dog food-orientated, which usually proves most helpful when training; it also discourages fussy eating.

Feeding guidelines

Here are some basic guidelines to follow when feeding your dog.

• Place a feeding mat, or newspaper, under feeding bowls, because many dogs are messy eaters.

• It is best to introduce changes to diet gradually to avoid digestive upsets.

• Never give spiced food or that to which any alcohol has been added.

• To prevent choking, remove all bones from fresh meats and fish.

• Fresh, clean drinking water should always be available.

• Make sure food and water bowls are always clean.

• Never allow your dog to eat chocolate intended for human consumption, as it is poisonous to them.

• Consult your vet if your dog shows any reluctance to eat or drink.

• Discourage your dog begging at the table, and certainly don't give into it. Sometimes it can be hard to resist those pleading eyes, but you must for the sake of your dog's waistline and health.

Food hygiene

• Canned foods deteriorate quickly once opened, so refrigerate and use within 24 hours. Decant leftover canned foods into ceramic, stainless steel or plastic food containers to avoid 'tin contamination'.

• Household disinfectants and detergents can taint food and water bowls and put your pet off using them, so it is preferable to use salt solution (1 teaspoon to half a litre/ 1 pint of water) or proprietary pet bowl cleaners, and then rinse thoroughly in clean water to clean and disinfect them. Clean bowls daily – your dog's good health depends on it.

• Wash pet feeding items separately from your own.

• When feeding semi-moist food, reseal the packet to make it airtight in order to retain freshness and reduce moisture loss until the next mealtime.

Feeding titbits from the table can lead to dogs actually thieving food from tables and work surfaces, so don't inadvertently encourage this habit as it is very difficult to break.

The right environment

For your dog to be mentally and physically healthy, he must feel safe and secure in his environment. If you are to remain unworried and be able to enjoy your pet to the full, you must be positive that you are doing all you can to keep him happy and protected from harm. Fulfilling your dog's essential needs within his environment (see the checklist) will help you both remain contented – and sane. As long as these needs are met, he will be a very happy dog.

Checklist

✓ safe, comfortable resting places
✓ sense of security
✓ safe territory
✓ personal space
✓ toys to satisfy hunting instincts
✓ ample food and water
✓ acceptable social interaction

Living accommodation

Ideally, you should live a house large enough to accommodate your family and your chosen size and type of dog, with plenty of space for everyone. If you don't have a suitably sized garden in which to adequately exercise him, then you must be prepared for two one-hour walks or so per day, with somewhere safe to exercise off-lead.

If house-proud, you must be prepared for a lot of extra work in keeping your home sweet-smelling and free of dog hairs and muddy paw prints. For minimal mess – and stress to all concerned – don't get a large, hairy, slobbery type of dog.

Avoid the temptation of being swayed by the appearance of dogs you have seen on TV and in magazines. Remember, you are buying a pet, not an accessory. It is no use thinking about a Great Dane, Afghan Hound, Border Collie, German Shepherd Dog or any other large working or herding breed if you live in a flat or small townhouse as these dogs don't thrive, mentally as well as physically, being 'cooped up'; they need plenty of room if they are to remain sane and sound.

By the same token, if you like the look of a pretty longhaired breed, such as the Lhasa Apso or Old English Sheepdog, but are not prepared to go to the trouble and expense of keeping its coat properly maintained, it won't stay healthy and looking good for long. Similarly, if you live in the country and are looking for a companion for long walks a Pekingese is not for you – they prefer the indoor, pampered life as the companion of a devoted owner.

If your home environment is not suited to the type of dog you have, then it is often a recipe for disaster. If you do your homework, however, and

Many people fancy a sports dog, like this English Springer Spaniel, for a pet, but live to regret their choice if they cannot provide enough exercise, training and mental stimulation for these animals.

Safe and secure

Just like you, your dog needs to feel secure in his world to remain calm and contented. Providing adequately for your pet's essential needs, mentally and physically, is the first step towards achieving this ideal. A feeling of security is enhanced by respecting your dog's personal space. Providing safe places where your dog can rest without being bothered by anyone (especially children when the dog has had enough of play) or another animal, or simply watch the world go by from a safe vantage point, is paramount to your dog's emotional well-being. Just as we like to have time by ourselves for a while – to be able to relax, be alone with our thoughts, or to sleep undisturbed to recharge our batteries – so too do dogs. Just as we are likely to become irritable if our personal space and time is invaded, so too are dogs. So the rule is to let sleeping dogs lie!

A 'sanctuary' where your dog knows he can go to rest undisturbed is essential for his mental and physical well-being.

choose your dog well for the type of environment you can offer him, then you have the best chance of enjoying a match made in heaven.

Home comforts

Important allowances for pet dogs include their own personal space comprising areas they can rest in undisturbed, toys that fulfil their hunting instincts through what we view as play, and, of course, sufficient food and water to satisfy their body needs (see pages 38–45).

As most people who keep dogs as pets want their animals to be close to them for the affection and company they provide, it stands to reason that the majority are kept in the home. To make your home as appealing as possible to your pet, meaning that the relationship between you both will be as successful and problem-free as possible, you must provide him with the facilities most important to him.

Your temperament

Another crucial consideration is how you relate to your dog. Whatever type of dog you choose, he will sense your emotions, so a stressed owner is likely to end up with a stressed pet. Dogs respond best to calm, consistent handling. Shouting at or hitting him will confuse and frighten him resulting, not surprisingly, in the development of behaviour problems.

A good owner is patient and controlled enough not to become angry at a dog if he does something you perceive as wrong. The old adage 'a poor workman blames his tools' is something you should bear in mind when owning a dog; if he does something inappropriate as far as you are concerned, then you have not trained him or catered for his needs adequately. In such cases, look to what may have caused the problem, and then rectify it to the best of your ability. Could it be that he is not receiving enough attention, exercise and so on? Find the root cause of the problem and you are halfway to finding the solution.

Be safe, not sorry

Not taking out appropriate insurance when you get a dog could prove false economy. It could mean being faced with a massive veterinary bill if your dog needs extensive treatment, while a lawsuit against you for personal or property damage caused by your dog could leave you facing financial ruin. Shop around for the best insurance deal and ask your vet for recommendations; then remember to read the small print on policy proposals.

Some dogs dislike being left at home alone while their owners are out at work, and suffer separation anxiety. This can lead to all sorts of behavioural problems, such as relieving themselves in the house, over-the-top attention-seeking, possessive aggression, barking or chewing – or all of these things.

Top tip

Swap toys around on a regular basis so that your dog does not become bored with them; doing so will keep his attention levels on them high. Some dogs prefer toys that roll, since they like a long chase, whereas others prefer toys that are shaped to bounce erratically or simulate the twists and turns of live prey.

Your lifestyle

If you work all day, you should consider getting a dog that will not mind this (and this is likely to be an adult, since it is not fair to leave puppies on their own for any length of time). Alternatively, you could arrange to have someone come and see to the dog at least once during your absence and let him out to relieve himself.

If you get a puppy, the first couple of months are going to be particularly time-consuming – you will need to spend time on house training and basic obedience training. Later, you will need to allow at least two hours every day for care and exercise. Are you able to devote this essential time to exercise, train and play with a dog? If not, rethink your reasons for getting one.

Boredom beaters

A filled Kong toy will help keep your dog occupied when you are not there. You can also use it to distract him when necessary.

1 *Fill the Kong with soft cheese or peanut butter. Push biscuit treats down into the soft filling.*

2 *Seal in the filling by smoothing it with a knife. Give the toy to your dog to enjoy!*

Playing with toys is the domestic dog's substitute for hunting; it helps to keep him mentally and physically fit.

Playtime

Establishing certain times when you can devote attention to your dog will soon become a regular routine he looks forward to, and make his attention-seeking a thing of the past. To make this quality time interesting and more fulfilling for both of you, invest in a selection of toys that your pet finds entertaining, and choose toys according to his perceived value of them; 'low-value' toys can be given for everyday use, while 'high-value' toys are extremely useful when training.

A suitably sized ball for your dog to chase and retrieve and an activity toy (such as a puzzle feeder, or stuffed Kong – see the panel opposite for how to do this) to keep him occupied will do fine to start with. Home-made toys can also include cardboard boxes filled with scrunched-up newspaper in which toys or food treats are hidden, while games you can play with your dog include hiding toys or treats around the house for him to find.

Should you wish to purchase a selection of low-value and high-value toys, there is a vast range specially designed for dogs available in pet stores to suit all pockets and types of dog. Bear in mind that strong-jawed dogs, such as Bull Terriers, soon destroy toys, so choose those that are durable (unless you have an unlimited budget).

Did you know ...?

Dogs with nothing to chase in their environment may resort to chasing the only thing that moves – their tail – and this can become an obsession (a 'stereotypy'; see page 63).

Interaction

Different dogs require different degrees of social contact with their owners and others of their own kind. Some will be more independent and aloof than their owners wish, while others need plenty of attention in order to thrive. Dogs that actively seek out human company show signs of distress if they cannot get enough.

Dogs that have a low need for social contact may learn to tolerate their owners' attention, but never seem to really

Top tip

Don't give your dog old items of clothing or footwear to play with, or he may view all such items, unwanted or not, as fair game.

enjoy it, so this desire must be recognized and accepted. For a person that requires an openly affectionate canine companion, this can be, understandably, disappointing, so it pays to research which breeds would be better suited.

Being social creatures, most dogs appreciate the company of their own kind on a regular basis to enact natural interaction. However many of the 'fighting' breeds simply do not get on amicably with strange dogs (males and females alike), or indeed even people, so beware of this when taking them out for walks; for safety's sake; such dogs should be muzzled when in public places, and in some countries this is, in fact, a legal requirement.

If you have a dog that simply does not get on with other dogs – and some don't – then again extreme caution should be taken when they are exercised in public places.

Environmental harmony

There are a couple of things to consider in order to achieve this ideal. The first is your dog's safety inside the house, in the garden and beyond, and the second is maintaining good relations with your neighbours.

Outdoor safety

Outdoor hazards include vehicular traffic, harassment from other dogs and humans, poisoning from harmful substances, and contracting diseases from other dogs.

• **Garden/yard security** Make sure your fence is dog-proof so that your pet cannot escape. Inspect fencing daily and secure any holes in hedging or fencing immediately. Some dogs are excellent athletes and can scale a 2m (6ft) fence with no problem, especially entire dogs keen to find a mate, so ensure your boundary enclosure is suitable for the type and character of dog you own.

• **Poisons** Keep garden chemicals (such as weedkillers and slug pellets) safely locked away where your dog cannot gain access to them. If you service the car, clean up any spilt antifreeze and oil; dogs find antifreeze appetizing and will lick it, while oil on fur or paws can result in poisoning if it is ingested when the dog grooms himself. Most dogs will instinctively avoid poisonous plants, both indoor and

Being with members of their own species is important to most dogs, so they should be allowed the opportunity to do so on a regular basis. Joining a properly conducted training class is an excellent way of achieving this.

Canine fact

Being originally bred to catch and kill small animals, such as rats, that were considered to be vermin, Terriers have strong predatory instincts. They, therefore, particularly enjoy playing with squeaky toys, as these simulate the squeaks of captured prey.

outdoor (such as laburnum and poinsettia), but puppies – being interested in everything – can occasionally fall victim to them. If you are worried about this danger then, if possible, remove any plants that may prove fatal if eaten by dogs – your vet can advise on the worst offenders.

Dogs can also suffer poisoning from eating contaminated food they have found, such as poisoned vermin carcasses. See page 159 for what to do if you suspect your dog has eaten something poisonous.

• **Toad poisoning** Dogs do tend to investigate frogs and toads, and catch the occasional one before they know any

A dog left outside in a pen all day with nothing to occupy him will soon become bored and resort to inappropriate behaviour, such as barking, to amuse himself.

Top tip

Don't throw sticks for dogs to chase and retrieve, nor encourage your pet to carry one. Prone to splintering, sticks can cause mouth and stomach injuries, while many an unfortunate dog has been impaled on the stick they were retrieving, resulting in grievous – even fatal – injuries.

better. Toads emit a vile-tasting, sometimes toxic, substance when under threat. Dogs react to this by shaking their head frantically, salivating and pawing at their mouth in an effort to rid themselves of the nasty, irritating substance. If you suspect toxic toad poisoning, consult your vet immediately.

• **Snake bites** Consult your vet immediately if you suspect your dog has been bitten by a poisonous snake.

Indoor safety

Although you think your home may be safe for your dog, there are in fact a number of potential hazards you need to be aware of for your pet's well-being.

• **Cleaning fluids and detergents** Make sure your dog does not have access to them.

Keep waste bins out of your dog's reach, otherwise he may scavenge and become injured through eating rubbish or being cut on cans.

• **Powder carpet fresheners** Dogs may suffer paw, skin and respiratory problems if these products are used.

• **Electric leads** These can prove fatal if chewed, but young, curious dogs often view them as irresistible play items. Keep wires to a minimum in those areas of the house where dogs are allowed.

• **Sewing materials** Keep needles, threads, buttons and elastic bands under lock and key.

• **Human medicines** Keep these locked away, so your dog does not have access to them.

• **Hot water** Keep your dog out of the bathroom while you are running a bath in case he jumps or falls into the hot water (and fatal incidences of this have been reported); for both human and animal safety, in any case, run the cold water first and add the hot to suit afterwards.

• **Noise** A dog's hearing is extremely sensitive and can easily be damaged, so don't subject him to loud sound from hi-fis or TV. In any case, loud sound of any kind is distressing to an animal.

Interaction

Be aware that rough play can lead to your dog becoming confused as to what behaviour is acceptable and what is not. For example, if you decide to get down on the floor and play-wrestle with the dog, then it is likely that he will try to dominate the situation. This often gets out of hand; his natural instincts come to the fore and this can result in injury to a member of the family, often with disastrous consequences for all concerned.

If this happens, it is usually the dog that gets the blame, yet it is not the dog's fault, but rather that of human failure to understand the behavioural boundaries between the two species. This is why it is so important to teach children, being more impulsive and less aware of what could happen, how to behave around pets of any kind. On this theme, do advise visitors of how to behave around your dog if you feel that their behaviour is not appropriate in the circumstances – for both their own and your pet's sake. If you are worried, put your dog in the garden.

Keeping everyone happy

Neighbours who object to a dog's barking can make life pretty unpleasant for both you and your pet, and understandably so – much as any person loves dogs, listening to a barking dog at all hours of the day can be extremely annoying.

If you keep your dog in a pen during the day when you are out, then, if this is possible, site the pen further away from neighbours, preferably with a wall to deaden the sound between the properties. If you cannot do this, then you will have to look at keeping the dog indoors and getting someone to come in to see to him while you are out.

Sometimes the use of a bark-activated spray collar can work well in these cases – when the dog barks, the collar sprays a harmless substance (either water or citronella-scented liquid) under the chin; the dog doesn't like it, and soon learns that barking results in this happening to him, so he remains quiet. However, do not use such a collar if there are two dogs kept together; if the wearer is not barking but the other is barking in close proximity, then the collar-wearer will be squirted and won't understand why, and this is unfair and cruel. Another ploy worth trying is to provide your dog with activity toys which will keep him entertained – and quiet – for hours.

Frequently asked question

Q What should I do if my dog goes missing?

A Dogs that are allowed outside to roam free are at risk of disappearing for any number of reasons, including being knocked down, being stolen, finding somewhere else to live, being mistaken as a stray and taken in by a well-meaning person or by a rescue centre. A missing pet could even result from him being stolen from you while you are walking him. The pain of not knowing what has happened to your pet when he does not come home can be devastating. If your dog goes missing there are several courses of action to take.
• Report the disappearance to the police, in case he has been found and handed in.
• Contact local authorities to see if there have been any dogs reported as being killed or injured on the roads.
• Contact local vets and rescue centres to see if your dog has been brought in. If your dog is microchipped or is wearing a collar and ID tag then he will be immediately identifiable.
• Ask neighbours if they have seen your dog and to check their gardens, outbuildings, sheds and garages.
• Put up 'Have you seen this dog?' posters in the neighbourhood shops, pet stores, schools and post offices (asking their permission to do so first) featuring a photo of your pet and a good description. Offering a reward can sometimes help bring about a speedy recovery.

If your dog persists in escaping the confines of your property boundary constructions, you are probably not providing enough stimulation to keep him occupied at home. Remember, too, that neutered dogs are more content with staying at home than entire ones.

• Because there is a ready black market for pedigree dogs, if yours is one then it is possible he has been stolen; contact the police and have a description of your pet at the ready.
• Contact a lost-and-found pet service to register your loss – if you have internet access you will find sources there if you key in 'lost pet' to a search engine. Failing that, vets and rescue centres can often provide contact telephone numbers for such services.
With luck, it won't be too long before you find your pet, or at least know what happened to him. When this happens, inform the people you told about his disappearance so that they do not continue to look for him.

Bringing your dog home

So that it runs comfortably and smoothly, and is free of stress for all concerned, you must prepare for the big event before you bring your new pet home. It is important to establish care rules and routine for all the family in advance of the big day when you will collect your dog. Setting a date well in advance will also give you time to get all the necessary items ready, shown in the checklist.

Checklist

✓ travelling crate/dog grille or harness
✓ bed and bedding, placed in quiet area
✓ food, water and bowls
✓ toys
✓ collar, ID tag and lead
✓ veterinary check-up appointment

When to collect your dog

For puppies, take a week or so off from work, as a young puppy will need feeding and letting out to relieve himself more frequently than an adult. Over this period of time, gradually train the puppy to wait a little longer between toilet times (adjusting feeding times appropriately to suit, since puppies usually want to go after eating). Gradually leave him longer and longer without your attention, or presence, restricted to an area of the house where he can do little damage and which is safe for him, to accustom him to being left on his own in preparation for when you go back to work. You will need to arrange for someone to come in and see to the puppy at least once during the day while you are out until he is older and can cope better mentally and physically with your prolonged absences.

If your new dog is an adult, arrange to collect him in the middle of a weekend so you have just one day before everyone goes out to work or school and the everyday routine begins. If you spend a week at home to settle him in, he will get used to having you around all the time and find it difficult to cope when normal life resumes.

Pre-arrival preparations

A couple of days before you collect a puppy, take the bedding he is to have at home to the breeder, or wherever you are getting him from, so the

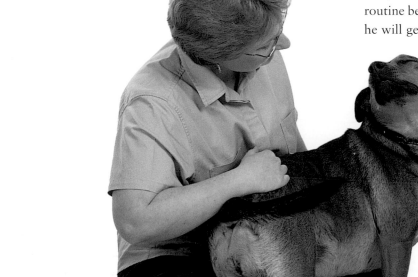

Let a new dog come to you when he is ready to do so – don't try to force him into interaction or you may frighten him, which will get the relationship off to a poor start. See pages 86–87 for detailed information on handling and interacting with a new pet.

puppy can use it there. This is so that the puppy's own smell, or that of his mother and litter mates, will transfer to the bedding and make him feel more at home in his new environment (both when travelling home and once ensconced in it). It is advisable to take two lots of bedding in case the puppy has an 'accident' on it, or when bringing him home.

Buy the equipment you will need (see pages 30–37), in particular a crate or sturdy carrier, depending on the size of the puppy, to transport him in. Find out from the breeder or owner what food the puppy is used to, so that you can get some. Ask how much he is being fed and how often. At the collection point, line the carrier or crate with the bedding you left there, put the puppy in and ensure the door is securely shut. Make sure you have all the paperwork necessary from the former owner (receipt, pedigree papers, registration and ownership transfer documents and vaccination certificate, as appropriate) before setting off.

For an adult dog, having ensured you have got all the appropriate equipment, you will need a crate, travel harness (if he is used to wearing one) or a dog grille to safely enclose the dog for his journey home.

Travelling home

Secure the carrier either on a seat with a seat belt, in the back of an estate vehicle, or in the footwell on the floor; a crate or travel harness should be placed in the rear of the car (but never in an enclosed boot or trunk). The inside of the vehicle should be of a moderate temperature with sufficient airflow so that the dog is comfortable in transit; too much heat can be fatal on long journeys. Offer water in a bowl at regular intervals if you are travelling any distance. Even if the dog protests at being enclosed all the way home, do not be tempted to let him out, for safety's sake; you or a passenger can talk to and reassure him, which may help him settle. Covering the crate with a blanket may help calm an excitable, barking dog.

On arrival home

Take the dog straight home (unless you have another dog – see 'Introducing other dogs' page 56) and walk him in the garden. Let him off the lead to run around and explore. Then take him inside, so he can explore the house for an hour or so. Make sure the family do not fuss over him, as

It's important that you put your new dog's bed in a place where he can rest undisturbed yet not feel excluded from the family group

this will cause him undue stress, and that children behave quietly and gently around him – do not let them handle him too much (even though they will, naturally, want to) until he has got used to them and does not view them as a threat.

Next, take him for a walk, or let him into the garden again and play a game with him, if appropriate, to begin the bonding process. After that, encourage him to go on his bed and rest for a while, leaving him undisturbed. Learning where his rest area is, and that he will be left in peace there, will help him settle.

See pages 74–79 for detailed information on socializing your new pet with other animals.

Canine fact

Dogs may be agitated and whine during the first few nights at their new home. Allowing them to stay in your bedroom, or just outside it, may help them to feel secure, and thus settle them; gradually move their bed away from you at nights until you have it in the place it is to be permanently.

Usually, an existing adult will accept a puppy without problems because the puppy does not represent a threat, but to be on the safe side it is best to follow the advice given under 'Introducing other dogs' .

Introducing other dogs

If you have an existing dog and are getting another adult, then it can be less stressful for all concerned to have them meet initially on neutral ground. For example, have a family member or a friend bring your dog to meet the new one on a walk (both on leads at first) to keep potential territorial argument to a minimum. Dogs that are of different sexes are likely to cause less upset.

Before bringing the new dog home, remove anything he and your existing pet are likely to fight over, such as toys and food bowls. Always be sure to pay attention to your existing pet first, so he doesn't feel excluded. Avoid situations that may cause aggravation between the two; for example, feed them separately at first, and do not leave them alone together until it is obvious they have become friends.

Settling in

While a puppy usually settles in very quickly and adapts to your routine well, an adult dog often takes longer. He will feel displaced and unsettled for a while, and you should try to give him the time and space he needs to adjust during that period. Try to be sympathetic to how he feels, but do not allow any bad habits to begin – such as allowing him to climb on furniture or receive titbits from the table – that you may later want to correct.

When taking your new dog/pup for a walk, keep him on the leash until you are confident he will come back immediately when called. A useful tip is to carry really

Top tip

Choose a vet as close to home as possible, so that you will be able to get the dog to the surgery quickly in an emergency.

Did you know ...?

Giving your new dog some activity toys to play with will help to keep him happily occupied and feel more at home, while feeding and play times together will help strengthen the bonding process between family members and the dog.

Frequently asked question

Q How soon after I get a dog should I take him for a health check?

A Wait until he has settled down, then take him to the vet to ensure he is fit and healthy and not suffering from any obvious ailments. Take him sooner if you are worried about anything. If you collect a puppy at 8 weeks he will need taking to the vet for his first course of vaccination (unless he has already received this), and then again at 10–12 weeks for his second, plus a developmental check. At the check-up, you can ask the vet about identity microchipping (which may be done there and then) and neutering if applicable.

smelly and tasty treats in your pocket, or in a bumbag around your waist, and let the dog know they are there. Let him sniff them, see where they are kept, and give him one every now and then, particularly when you feel his attention wandering away from you. Most dogs will stick to your side like glue if they know you have prized titbits.

To help establish hierarchy rules, always feed your new dog after the family has eaten and do not allow him to 'hound' you at the table.

CANINE BEHAVIOUR

Many dogs are treated badly or inappropriately simply because their owners are ignorant of what their pets are telling them. Dogs have a language all of their own, but, if we observe them carefully, we can build up a detailed picture of their body language and actions that helps us guess how they might be feeling, what they want from us, and what they need. By making an effort to learn what your dog is saying to you, you will understand him better and therefore be able to give him an improved quality of life.

Body language

Dogs employ a vast range of facial expressions, vocal sounds and body postures in order to communicate. Many owners talk to their dogs, and sometimes the two parties appear to understand each other. Dogs possess a large universal vocabulary, and some people have attempted to translate what they are saying. You can also learn to recognize some of what your dog is communicating if you observe the points on the checklist carefully.

Checklist
✓ watch
✓ listen
✓ learn
✓ understand

Calm, content and curious

The pricked ears and kind, interested expression indicates a calm, content and curious dog. This breed, the German Shepherd Dog, was developed in its native country to herd sheep, so its natural instincts are to guard and be watchful, and the expression here shows the breed at its best – alert, generous and intelligent.

Unhappy or ill

This body posture indicates a depressed and unhappy dog. Such a stance could be due to a stressful atmosphere (a perceived threat from another dog, a disruptive household or physical or mental abuse) or because he is experiencing physical discomfort due to illness.

Fear-aggression

This is the face of fear and defensive aggression. The ears are back and the mouth is wide with worry. However, the lips are drawn slightly up to expose the teeth, the head is up ready to bite and the eyes are fixed on the antagonist so that further aggressive action can be taken if necessary. This face is accompanied by a series of explosive barks designed to make the aggressor move away.

Frightened

A frightened dog will pull away from whatever it is that has worried him: the tail and ears are tucked well out of harm's way in case of attack, eyes are fixed on whatever is scaring him in case he needs to flee quickly, and the whites of the eyes show, indicating that the eyes are wide open to gather more information. The heart will be racing and body preparing itself for a fast getaway.

Aggressive

This is a deliberate display of strength and the 'adversary' is being given the chance to back down, but any retreat must be slow and obvious to avoid an attack. This expression is designed to show the dog's impressive weaponry – his teeth. The lips are drawn up as far as they will go, which means that the corners of the mouth are brought forward rather than drawn back as in a fearful dog.

Playful

This is the signal that says 'I would like to play with you'. Dogs will give this signal to humans as well as to other dogs and animals. This pose will be held for a few seconds, with the tail beating furiously, before the dog jumps up and runs off, looking over his shoulder to see if his invitation to chase has been successful. Many dogs do this as a greeting and 'smile' to show that a person he knows is coming near.

Uneasy

This dog's body stance and posture shows that he is scared and very uneasy with nowhere to hide or feel really safe. He is waiting miserably for better options to become available, his ears lifted to alert him to the tiniest sound indicating what is to happen next.

Investigative

Sniffing people, other animals and anything else in his environment is the dog's way of finding out vital information about whether something is friend, foe, good to eat, what sex it is or if it is ready to mate. Owners carry all sorts of scents on their clothes, especially if they have been with or near other dogs or animals, so a dog will naturally want to investigate those smells. In the absence of any interesting smells, dogs often sniff the human groin area to take in the scent of the person they are investigating, which can be very embarrassing for owners and visitors who don't appreciate the intrusion!

Wary

This is not a good way to greet an unfamiliar dog. Dogs, especially those that have been ill treated in the past, find this kind of approach worrying and try to shrink away from the 'threat', with their ears back (to protect them in case of attack), eyes wide open (to see the threat better) and their tail tucked between their legs (to keep it out of harm's way). Putting your hands towards and making eye contact with an unknown dog may well be perceived as a potential attack.

Submission

Rolling on the back, exposing the belly and leaving himself vulnerable displays a dog's acceptance of a higher-ranking individual. This strategic positioning is a good one to get the dog out of a situation in which he would otherwise receive punishment.

Submissive 'grinning'

A submissive 'grin' like this is often misinterpreted by humans, who think the dog is being aggressive. In reality, these 'grins' are similar to a human smile and are often shown when the dog is greeting people he knows or when he is being admonished. These 'grins' are usually reserved for humans rather than other dogs, and the propensity to show them seems to be inherited and to run in families.

Barking

Barking is the dog's way of speaking and is used to sound an alarm and warn other pack members (human or animal) of intruders, as an effective way of warning off potential foes and also to indicate a state of high excitement, such as during play.

Listening

Cocking the head on one side is a way of turning the ears to better pinpoint the direction and source from which a sound is coming.

Howling

Howling is a good way to communicate with others who are far away. If separated from the pack (human or other dogs), howling and waiting for others to respond helps the lost one to know in which direction to travel to rejoin them. Dogs kept in kennels, and sometimes those left alone in the house all day while their owners are out, will often howl as if to reunite themselves with members of their lost pack.

Yawning and licking lips

Yawning and flicking their tongue in and out is often one of the first signs that your dog is uneasy about a situation. He may be in conflict within himself, trying to decide whether to move away, or he could be signalling to you that he is not happy about something. Humans frequently mistakenly think the dog is tired and take no notice of this important signal.

Begging or attention-seeking

Many dogs learn that lifting a paw at, or even pawing or nosing, a person is a guaranteed way of getting attention or a titbit. This dog's head is up and his senses focused on whatever it is he is trying to get, indicating confidence and determination. On the other hand, a dog that lifts his paw but with head lowered (indicating that his teeth are out of action) is being submissive.

Resting and relaxed

Dogs who sleep with their eyes closed and body totally relaxed indicate they feel safe in their surroundings. Dogs who sleep with one eye open and an ear half-cocked are not relaxed enough to sleep fully and are ready for further action in case there is the option of something more exciting to do.

Obsessive behaviour

Also known as a 'stereotypy', a dog that displays obsessive behaviour does so because the habit has become ingrained – a good example of this is a zoo animal pacing or rocking backwards and forwards. This gives them something to do and some kind of comfort. In dogs, an example of stereotypical behaviour is chasing their tails, and they become oblivious to everything around them as they circle and spin. Sometimes they catch it and make it bleed, but the important part to them is the chase – even if their tail is amputated, they will continue to pursue the stump. Providing a more stimulating environment and more games with toys can provide the dog with a more fulfilling life, negating the need for them to engage in obsessive behaviours. Causes of stereotypical behaviour include:
• being in a regularly frightening situation (such as in an abusive environment)
• frustration
• anticipation (for example, at feeding or exercise times)
• a mismatch between the environment and the dog
• environmental imperfection (where something is required and not received)
• the dog misunderstanding what is required of him
• isolation (lack of contact with humans or other animals

The wolf in your home

Wolves, the ancestors of our pet dogs, are social animals that enjoy each other's company. Humans have taken this trait and bred selectively over the generations so that the dogs we have in our homes are generally very sociable and loyal. However, it must never be forgotten that dogs evolved as pack animals that had to compete with others and kill prey to survive, and these traits are still there beneath the surface of domesticity. This mix of 'wild' and 'domesticated' has contributed to the fascinating canine character we know today. The dog's main character traits appear on the checklist.

Checklist

✔ dependence
✔ affection
✔ opportunism
✔ instinctiveness
✔ cunning
✔ being predatory
✔ competitiveness
✔ stealth
✔ possessiveness
✔ assertiveness
✔ following a hierarchy
✔ playfulness

Domestic dogs are pack animals, just like the wolves they are descended from, who become depressed and behave in a manner that is unacceptable to us if denied social contact.

Instincts will out! Since passing on genes to the next generation is important, fights between rival male dogs can turn nasty if allowed to continue. Here, while the Weimaraner (the grey dog) is occupied trying to pin one of his rivals to the ground, the sandy-coloured dog makes the most of his chance to practise mounting behaviour. Being young, he is no match for these two but, excited by the competition, he seizes the opportunity to outdo the dog he thinks will be the most likely victor.

Did you know ...?

Apart from domestic dogs *Canis familiaris*, there are 36 recognized species of the Canidae family, including:

• wolves • foxes • coyotes • jackals • dingoes

Where dogs came from

Dogs were in existence before the earliest human. According to fossil evolution, the origins of our dogs can be traced back about 40 million years to a small carnivorous mammal called Miacis. This tiny weasel-like creature gradually evolved to produce, some 10 million years ago, the forerunners of present-day canids, called Cynodesmus and Tomoritus. From them, the evolution of the canid line continued up to about 10,000–12,000 years ago when wolves – along with foxes, jackals and coyotes – appeared in the form they are today. Today's dog is derived from four types of wolf (*Canis lupus*): the northern grey wolf, the pale-footed Asian wolf, the small desert wolf of Arabia and the woolly-coated wolf of Tibet and northern India. This information was determined in 1935 by R.I. Pocock, who suggested that these four types of wolf contained the genes necessary to develop all modern breeds of dog.

Trained sheepdogs are highly prized for their skills, both practically and in competitions.

Modern dogs

Domestication occurred when humans as we know them came on the scene. However, 'modern' man's ape-like predecessors had already been co-existing with dog-like creatures for thousands of years before this time. Various archaeological finds around the world support the theory that domestication (the beginning of selective breeding to produce required types of dog) probably occurred around 10,000–12,000 years ago in different parts of the globe rather than in one place. In Israel, for example, a fossil find dating back to then revealed the skeleton of a puppy and a young male human, with his hand upon the puppy's head, apparently in a gesture of affection. In the USA, evidence of the early domestication process has been discovered in the State of Idaho's Beaverhead mountains.

The first domesticated dogs

Several theories exist as to how dogs were first domesticated in response to human needs.

Hunting help

The first is that dogs were originally used by humans to help with hunting, in that the humans would scare off wolves from their kills and scavenge the remains. Perhaps by means of training orphaned wolf cubs, humans might have begun to employ wolves' hunting skills more directly.

Food source

A second theory, though unlikely, is that humans hunted wolves for food and, in times of plenty, took back orphaned cubs as children's playthings.

Companion pets

A third theory is that, right from the start, dogs were pets or companions rather than a food source or working animals. It is easy to see how children might have reared orphaned wolfcubs as pets, with perhaps the cubs later being utilized as working animals as a greater depth of understanding developed between them and their human owners.

Guard dogs

The fourth theory is that early domestic dogs were used for guarding rather than for hunting, due to their superior senses of hearing and smell alerting humans to unnoticed danger threatening their homesteads. This guarding could then have been extended to use with flocks of sheep and cattle, since humans soon began to domesticate both of these as well.

Mutual benefits

A fifth theory is that humans did not actively domesticate the dog, but that a relationship developed between them for mutual advantage. Dogs hung around homesteads scavenging for food humans had discarded, as well as hunting rats and other species that lived on grain stored by humans. Tamer individuals that were thought useful in keeping down vermin may have been tolerated and then befriended by humans. The friendship would then have developed, leading to the dog becoming the worker and companion of today.

Living with man

Cave drawings discovered in the Pyrenees from the Upper Palaeolithic period (after the last Ice Age, some 10,000–12,000 years ago) show bowmen and dogs co-operating in a hunt. What is interesting is that the dogs depicted are of a lightly built and long-legged conformation, with pricked ears and pointed muzzles, very similar to the wolves which then inhabited southern Europe, but possessing differences which show that humans were beginning to select the 'dogs' best suited to their purpose, and that the favoured type differed slightly from wild stock.

Around 5,000 years ago, humans were ceasing to be nomadic hunters, and beginning to make permanent settlements and farm the land. This in turn led to humans further developing types of dog suited to various tasks, such as herding and guarding, and not just exclusively for hunting. As humans became more prosperous, they could afford, and were also perhaps more disposed, to keeping dogs which did not perform any useful purpose apart from being simply pets and companions whose appearance and/or temperament were pleasing. Humans became a race of dog breeders and learned to produce dogs of all sizes and shapes able to accomplish a wide variety of tasks – from the huge Mastiff-like war dogs of the Babylonian Empire to the fleet-footed hunting and sport hounds bred by the Assyrians some 2,000 years later.

In more recent times, dogs were used to accompany carriages, hunt, flush game for sportsmen (and still do), provide 'entertainment' fighting pits for gamblers (now

Owner beware – even the smallest, cutest dog is a wolf in disguise, retaining the same instincts.

outlawed in western society), be pampered lap dogs for the elite, and drag loads (such as sleds).

Gradually, as the twentieth century matured, many of the traditional canine uses were phased out, to be replaced with nothing more than humans' desire to keep dogs as pets, and in the modern working roles of helpers for physically and mentally disabled people and in law enforcement. In many ways, dogs continue to contribute to the quality of our lives.

It is unlikely that the exact process of domestication will ever be fully known. Probably the relationship built up through a combination of reasons, and it may have started in slightly different ways in different geographical areas. As time went on, the wolf offspring must have come to live and grow in the closest possible association with humans, learning to respond to moods and obey commands.

Normal behaviour

Dogs display a number of traits that humans find annoying, strange or even disgusting (eating faeces is a prime example). Yet dogs do what they do for a reason. As far as they are concerned, they are doing nothing wrong, and they become confused when we scold them. Knowing why dogs do certain things will enable you to cope better with them as they occur. Such types of behaviour include those on the checklist.

Checklist

✓ vocal communication
✓ guarding and possession
✓ marking territory
✓ hierarchical behaviour patterns
✓ curiosity
✓ personal hygiene
✓ eating habits
✓ chase drive
✓ sleeping habits
✓ social interaction behaviours

Vocal communication

Compared to humans, dogs have a limited ability to communicate using sound and tend to rely more on body language to get their message across. The range of sounds they produce tends to be used to back up their body language rather than in isolation. Howling and growling are the least common sounds, but barking is used frequently, often in different ways to convey different meanings. These can range from guarding barks to those designed to get attention, or barking can be used just to let off steam during excitement, or when feeling frustrated.

Top tip

You can gauge the mental state of a dog from his posture, facial and vocal expressions, and as you get used to your own pet you will learn his own individual communication techniques. Generally, a stiff stance with jerky movement indicates aggression, uncertainty and fear, while a relaxed body and smooth movement denote a dog at ease.

Guarding and possession

Natural instinct dictates that to let another take away food will result in hunger. This principle sometimes gets transferred to toys and other items a dog possesses; to give them up is a sign of weakness. Guarding food or a toy, by growling or snapping at anyone who approaches to potentially take it away, is a dog's way of saying 'this is mine and you are not having it'. However, this line of defence is inappropriate in a human environment. In pet dogs, not letting go of something must be discouraged from an early age, otherwise aggression problems may later result. It is

Barking to get attention is common in pampered small dogs when they feel their owners are ignoring them. If their owners respond, they will stop; if not, they can continue in this way for an annoyingly long time.

There is no mistaking the intentions of this dog. He is top dog in the pack and one of his subordinates has been brave enough to question his authority. This dog's body is in a formidable posture, accompanied by a deep, rumbling growl, and he is ready to attack if the potential rival does not back down.

fine to let a non-aggressive or non-possessive dog occasionally win the toy in a tug game so as to keep his play motivation high, but make sure this is the exception and not the rule.

Hierarchical behaviour patterns

A pet dog often instinctively wants to become 'top dog' in a household 'pack'. This is because the strongest animals get the best food, the most comfortable sleeping places and the chance to breed and pass on their genes to the next generation. Dogs in a wild pack live in a social hierarchy in which they arrange themselves in status order beneath the leader. Good leaders look after the pack, making sure they are well fed and comfortable. They don't always give in to demands, and can be uncompromising and tough when necessary to maintain authority. They decide what to do and when to do it. They have sufficient strength to earn respect rather than constantly harassing or bullying the pack to stay in control.

In domestic circumstances, you must remember that you are the leader and your dog is the lower-status pack member. If the status alters, you will certainly have

Tail-wagging explained

A wagging tail does not always indicate a friendly and happy dog. You have to take into account the rest of his body language before deciding whether he is a friend or a foe. Wagging a raised, stiff tail implies tension and potential aggression, while wagging a low tail, possibly between his legs, indicates a fearful and/or submissive dog. Energetically wagging at half-mast is usually a good sign as, generally, it means the dog is neither tense nor depressed. As well as the wag, look at the dog's hackles (the top of the shoulder, just behind the neck), his body stance and facial expressions. If his hackles are raised (the hair will be stood up and bushed out), he is stiff-legged and has a fixed-eye expression, then this indicates to a person, or another animal, that the dog is on his guard and ready to attack if he deems it necessary. If the wagging tail comes complete with a relaxed body stance, 'smiley' face and lolling ears, then the dog is not looking for confrontation, but rather to play or receive some attention.

Frequently asked question

Q Why does my dog sometimes scrape his bottom along the ground?

A When a dog scrapes his bottom along the ground, propelling himself forward with his fore legs, this 'scooting' action indicates that he is suffering discomfort in his anal area. This could be due to worms, blocked anal glands, constipation or soreness. Such behaviour requires veterinary attention to determine the cause and provide a solution.

Some owners get annoyed when their dog sniffs around things too much, but this is their main way of finding out about the world, in the same way that we find out what is happening in our immediate environment by using our primary sense of sight.

problems in controlling your dog's behaviour. However, if this happens, all is not lost: the hierarchy in a wild dog pack is not fixed and will change if circumstances alter. Consequently, there is hope for humans whose dog has taken control of them. (See pages 88–91 for how to handle your dog.)

Chase drive

Humans have domesticated dogs and selectively bred them until they no longer resemble their wild ancestors, but they still retain many of the characteristics that make them efficient hunters. The hunting sequence can be broken down into components – scent-trail, watch, stalk, chase, grab, bite, shake, kill, consume – all of which can be seen in our own docile pets.

Top tip

Digging indicates that the dog is looking for food or for quarry to chase, catch and eat. Hunting dogs and terriers are particularly prone to digging in areas that their sense of smell tells them will be rewarding; so, unless you want your garden rearranged, reserve a special area in which your dog can indulge in this harmless habit. If you bury a toy or a bone in this special spot, your dog will get a reward for his efforts and will keep returning to it to try his luck again.

Different breeds of dog have been bred to exploit different elements of the hunting sequence: hounds are bred to track and trail, herding dogs to chase and terriers to catch and kill. If this strong desire to chase things is not channelled into acceptable working behaviour or games with toys, dogs can pick up bad habits and get into trouble for carrying out inappropriate chases (such as pursuing other animals, cars, joggers or cyclists).

Information gathering

Your dog can find out a lot by sniffing the urine and faeces left by other dogs. Although this procedure may be repellent to us, your dog can use it to discover who was recently in the area. Scents linger for some time once they have been laid and, to a dog, sniffing is like watching a video of all the things that may have happened in that place in the past.

Aggression

Dogs will only attack with intent if they deem it absolutely vital for their own well-being: in the wild, harming another pack member is only ever done as a last resort, because having an incapacitated dog means that there is one fewer to go out to find food and to guard the group as a whole.

In 'squaring up', the dog on the left is displaying the attitude of being 'armed to attack'; his hackles are raised, his teeth are bared and his body stance tense, ready to propel him into defence against an apparently hostile approach from another.

Interaction with others

A dog that presents no threat to humans and other animals tends either to ignore them completely, as if they were not there, or to greet them with his body totally relaxed and not tense as it would be if he were about to display aggressive behaviour. His tail will wag in a wide sweeping movement from side to side, and his facial expression will be one of a happy, silly 'grin', or of calm contentment (see page 60). Licking whoever he is greeting is an appeasement gesture that the dog uses to signal that he is no threat. He does this in the hope that whoever it is won't attack him.

Sleeping

Dogs spend quite a lot of time sleeping, especially as they get older, but do not necessarily sleep all night as we generally expect them to do in our homes. Providing puppies and young dogs with something to do when they wake up (such as leaving them toys to play with) can help

Attempting to lick a person's face has its origins in the behaviour of puppies in the wild who lick the mouths of adult dogs returning to the nest to get them to regurgitate food they are carrying in their stomachs. Allowing your dog to lick your face is not something that should be encouraged because of hygiene and safety reasons, especially where children are concerned.

prevent you suffering disturbed sleep. Many dogs prefer to sleep underneath some sort of protection, such as a table or bed, or behind a sofa. This could be linked to the trait of 'going to ground' in times of danger when puppies were raised in dens.

Playing

Generally, dogs are highly social creatures and love nothing more than the company of other dogs and to play silly games with them. However, whether or not two dogs will get on depends on how compatible their personalities are and how they are introduced.

Some dogs are shy and worried about others, whereas some are outgoing and are happy to meet as many other dogs as possible. As with people, some dogs are good at communication, but others often get into fights and squabbles because of confusion over their intentions. Signalling and body language play a large part in these encounters, and indicate how well a dog has been socialized with other dogs during and since puppyhood.

Personal hygiene

Few owners enjoy the sight of a dog using his tongue to clean his private places, but it is essential to realize that this is a necessary part of attending to his personal hygiene. Most dogs are very efficient at keeping themselves clean

Did you know ...?

Some dogs seem to love drinking from dirty puddles, or even slime-covered ponds, much to their owners' horror. It is wise not to let them do so, because the water could harbour parasites or be polluted with chemicals. Beware, also, when preparing your car for winter – dogs seem to find spilt antifreeze quite irresistible, but it is deadly poisonous to them.

without any help from humans, apart from those with gastric ailments resulting in diarrhoea (especially longhaired dogs), obese dogs who cannot reach their nether regions and older dogs who are not very flexible. It is important that you attend to these dogs' hygiene needs and wash their anal and genital areas, especially in hot weather when there are lots of flies about, otherwise soiled areas may become infested with maggots.

Scavenging

Most pet dogs get food handed to them at least once a day and never have to find their own food. Humans often feel that, because of this, there is no need for dogs to hunt or scavenge, and often punish them for doing so. However,

Eating grass or faeces

Eating grass aids your dog's digestion. When we get indigestion, we take an antacid; when dogs feel nauseated, they eat grass to induce vomiting and rid their stomach of whatever ails them. Eating grass in excess should be investigated by a vet. Eating and rolling in other animals' faeces is a habit most owners find repulsive. To a dog, however, eating faeces provides essential nutrients that his own body lacks, while rolling in them (and also on dead animals) is an instinctive way of masking his own scent in preparation for 'hunting'.

Urinating against posts and defecating on or next to another dog's motions is a highly effective 'messaging service'. The scent left behind in their 'calling cards' tells other dogs just who has passed that way, what sex they are and how big they are – hence the reason for male dogs aiming to leave their excretions as high as possible.

until we breed dogs that have very little remaining of the genetics of their ancestors, dogs will continue to have the drives and desires that allowed their predecessors to acquire enough to eat. Dogs can be trained not to raid the kitchen bin; in the case of a confirmed scavenger, however, the simplest thing to do is to make sure the bin is not kept where he has access to it.

Five steps to successful integration

1 Learn how to interpret your dog's body language, and so recognize his state of mind; remember that tail-wagging does not mean a dog is friendly.

2 A 'tense' body indicates uncertainty, fear or potential aggression, while a 'soft' body stance and movement denotes a relaxed, happy dog.

3 Remember how a dog's natural instincts dictates his behaviour, and learn how to work with this.

4 Find out the different breeds' inherent traits and use this knowledge to determine your ideal canine companion.

5 Remember not to get cross with your dog, but simply prevent him from doing the things that could be ultimately harmful to him by distracting him with a game or toy, or by not putting him in risky situations.

Did you know …?

Scratching up grass with the front and back legs after urinating and, more commonly, defecating, is another way of marking territory: odours left by the scent glands in the feet, along with the visual sign of disturbed earth, alert other animals to the dog's presence in that area. Another theory is that this scratching indicates that the dog is displaying relief having finished emptying its bladder or bowels. There is an air of satisfied finality about this action; possibly indicating the dog is no longer vulnerable to attack while relieving himself.

Socializing

Dogs must be well socialized, preferably from a very early age, if they are to accept humans, the domestic environment in which they live and other dogs and animals without any kinds of problem behaviour occurring. The checklist details all the things you need to introduce your dog to and encourage him to accept.

Checklist

- ✓ humans
- ✓ other dogs
- ✓ cats and other livestock
- ✓ traffic
- ✓ people making deliveries
- ✓ household appliances
- ✓ different environments
- ✓ travelling in the car
- ✓ staying in boarding kennels
- ✓ going to the vet
- ✓ being groomed by you or others

Social contact

Dogs are very social creatures. Different breeds of dog will enjoy the company of people and other animals to different extents, but all like to live their lives in a pack with others, whether human or canine. If denied social contact, they can become very depressed or 'badly behaved'. An undersocialized dog can be a real nightmare to live with, handle and control, so you need to socialize your pet properly for the safety and contentment of all concerned. See pages 76–77 for how to teach social skills and page 75 for a checklist of things to introduce your dog or puppy to.

Taking your dog to introduction classes where he can socialize with other humans and dogs will help teach him how to behave appropriately in the company of others.

Teach children to give the dog treats, both by hand and also by adding them to his dish while he is eating a meal, so that he views their hands as rewarding and not as a threat. Supervise children while they do this to be on the safe side. See pages 88–89 for detailed information on dogs and children.

Human contact

Dogs need to be taught to behave well around humans of all ages, colours, creeds, shapes and sizes. Examples of these include the following:

- the disabled and infirm
- spectacle-wearers
- wheelchair users
- babies and toddlers
- energetic teenagers
- noisy people
- timid people
- headdress-wearers
- uniform-wearers
- joggers
- cyclists, rollerbladers and skateboarders
- people pushing prams
- people carrying umbrellas
- people with beards and unusual hairstyles

It is a fact that many dogs have a problem with delivery people, due to territorial aggression (a form of fear-aggression). A properly socialized dog, after warning you that they are there, will be pleased to see people rather than want to see them off – providing they do not pose a threat to him or to you.

Delivery people come to the house and then, from the dog's point of view, go as soon as they are barked at. Not only are they entering your dog's territory, where he is most confident, but there will probably have been many occasions where they have entered your property, startled him into barking, and then gone away – often after doing something unusual such as pushing an envelope through the letter box.

To prevent aggression towards delivery people, make a point of introducing your dog to them, and getting them to give him treats or even throwing a toy for him, so that he views them as rewarding and so welcomes them.

Different environments

Things that are normal to us in our everyday environment both inside and outside the home can be confusing, even frightening, to a dog if he has not been properly introduced to and socialized with them. Items such as a vacuum cleaner, slippery floors, stairs, traffic, hair-drier, the television and washing machine can all be sources of mental distress to a dog.

Get your dog used to such things gradually but persistently, using lots of treats and games so that he views them as rewarding experiences. If your dog has grown up in

It is preferable to introduce a dog to other animals while he is still a young puppy, as he will then accept them as part of the norm, or part of the family, and not see them as strange creatures that warrant potentially trouble-making investigation.

a busy household, then he is more likely to view household appliances with indifference, but an older dog unused to them needs careful introductions in short training sessions so as not to overface him.

Livestock

Dogs need to be taught not to chase and attack creatures, such as other small household pets (for example rabbits and hamsters), chickens, sheep, horses and cattle. Always put your dog on the leash when walking him near livestock – for his safety and that of the animals. Remember that some farmers will shoot first and ask questions later if they see loose dogs near their livestock.

How to socialize your dog

Socialize your dog at his own pace. Rushing this process can result in him becoming nervous and timid, or even aggressive, or it could make formed behaviour problems worse, rather than alleviating them. Make introductions to new experiences short and sweet so that your dog views them as good things. Here are some examples.

Going to the vet

Take your dog just for a cuddle and a treat from your vet, so that he doesn't associate going to the vet with purely unpleasant experiences, such as injections.

Frequently asked question

Q I want to socialize my dog with other animals, but after a bad experience with my last dog I don't feel confident about how to go about it and handle my dog on my own. What can I do?

A Some good training schools hold introduction classes where dogs can meet other livestock – and these are well worth going to, as such introductions can be much more successful in a controlled environment where there is help on hand if you need it. You may have to travel quite a distance to find such a class, but it should be a valuable experience for both you and your dog.

If behaviour problems with your dog arise, a pet behaviour counsellor can provide experienced, practical help and advice. Your vet may be able to refer you to a reputable practitioner if necessary.

Car travel

Feed your dog in the car, or have games in it with the doors open (parked in a safe, off-road place) to begin with, so that your dog sees the car as a nice thing to be in. Then make initial journeys very short, ending with going for an enjoyable walk before returning home.

Staying in boarding kennels

Take your dog to the kennels to meet the staff and to play games with him there. Then take him again another day and leave him for an hour or so, with a toy and his bed for familiarity, before picking him up again, so that he learns that you will come back for him. Progress to a day, and then an overnight stay.

Being groomed

Accustom your dog to being regularly groomed by you and other family members, and friends if possible, so that if he needs to go to a grooming parlour and be groomed by strangers it won't be so much of a problem for him. Take him to the parlour for an initial visit to meet the staff, then when he goes for the real thing he is more likely to feel comfortable about it. Some parlours don't mind you staying while your dog is being groomed, but some dogs are better behaved when their owners are not there!

Canine fact

Agility classes are a great way of socializing dogs with other people and their dogs. Most dogs get so excited, and intent on what they are doing, that they forget to be wary or hostile, and instead find themselves thoroughly enjoying the interaction with other human and canine friends.

SOCIALIZATION PROGRAMME

Age	6–7 weeks	7–8 weeks	8–9 weeks	9–10 weeks
Adults (men and women)				
Young adults				
Middle-aged adults				
Elderly people				
Disabled/infirm				
Loud, confident people				
Shy, timid people				
Delivery people				
Joggers				
People wearing uniforms				
People wearing hats				
People with beards				
People wearing glasses				
People wearing motorbike helmets				
Children				
Babies				
Toddlers				
Juniors				
Teenagers				
Other animals				
Dogs – adults				
Dogs – puppies				
Cats				
Small pets				
Livestock				
Horses				
Environments				
Friend's house				
Shopping centre				
Park				
Outside a school				
Outside a children's play area				
Country walks				
Other				
Bicycles				
Motorbikes				
Traffic				

10–11 weeks	11–12 weeks	3–6 months	6–10 months

Socialization

Use this handy chart to monitor your dog's socialization progress as he meets each element contained within it. You can customize the chart as regards your dog's age as necessary, such as agility classess, dustcarts, trains, buses, large vehicles, ice cream vans, tractors or horse riders. Put a tick in the box for each example as your pet is introduced to each element – entering as many ticks per box as possible (indicating how many encounters your dog has had) – and expanding on his reaction, and if anything needs to be worked on further, in a diary kept for the purpose. This way you can keep an accurate track of your dog's progress. Take care not to overwhelm your pet; take things at his pace. Some areas may need more acclimatizatin than others, so be prepared for this – but remember that time and patience really do work wonders.

Remember that it is essential your dog sees these encounters as good and not bad ones, otherwise they could scare him and make him resistant to coping with them in a positive way, so ensure that each meeting is made as pleasant for him as possible – the use of food or toy rewards as he meets and greets each element are a good way of ensuring he views the encounters as rewarding, therefore non-threatening.

Promoting health and happiness

It's important to realize that pets need appropriate care as they are unable to live their lives as nature intended – that is to say, free to eat, drink, socialize, breed, source their own environment, sleep and exercise at will. They are totally dependent upon us to ensure they remain mentally and physically comfortable and healthy throughout their lives.

A happy and healthy dog is the product of a good owner who cares properly for their pet all through his life. This entails:

• ensuring that your dog has a balanced diet appropriate to his life stage

• making sure he is vaccinated against the diseases to which he is vulnerable

• only breeding from your dog if you can be as certain as possible that the resulting puppies will be of normal conformation and healthy, and that caring permanent homes can be found

• having your dog neutered if your pet is not to be kept for breeding purposes

• accommodating your dog's normal behaviour traits

• suitably addressing any 'abnormal' behaviour traits

• having the time and facilities to care for your pet properly

• taking your pet to the vet when he is unwell

• keeping the dog throughout his life, unless for any reason this is impossible

• grooming your pet and attending to parasite control as appropriate

• establishing a routine that your dog is comfortable with

• always treating your dog with respect and consideration

• never using physical punishment, as your dog will not understand why you are treating him in that way

• not relying on your dog for emotional support, as this is detrimental to his physical and mental health

• identifying your dog's likes and dislikes

In order to enjoy a successful partnership with your dog, you need to work at building a loving relationship built on mutual respect.

Did you know ...?

Dogs feel more at ease within a laid-back household where the atmosphere is calm and peaceful. Animals are quick to feel tension in an atmosphere and become unsettled by it, sometimes to the extent of becoming withdrawn, fearful and/or suffering ill health.

Can you afford a dog?

The average dog lives for around 12 years, which is a long time to commit mentally, physically and financially to another creature. Apart from the initial expense of buying your dog, neutering and essential equipment you will need, regular financial outlays include:

• food
• routine vaccinations
• veterinary check-ups
• internal and external parasite treatments
• holiday boarding/care fees
• health and third party/public liability insurance
• training classes
• replacement equipment as necessary
• specialized grooming care for certain coats (contact a grooming parlour before getting the dog of your choice and asking how much professional coat care will cost so you don't get an unpleasant shock later on)

Rehoming your dog?

It is possible that, for various reasons, you are finding it hard to devote enough time to exercising and training your dog, and consequently he has developed various behaviour problems that you simply cannot cope with. He is miserable, and so are you. The dog's welfare is foremost, so if there is nothing you can implement quickly and easily to solve the situation you are in, then finding the dog a home with someone who can offer the type of environment and training he needs is not a failure on your part: rather, it is a selfless act that will give the dog the chance to lead a more fulfilled and happier life. Rescue and rehoming centres may be able to provide you with useful information on how to go about finding the home your dog would be most comfortable with. Some rescue centres will even rehome your dog for you, providing you give them a donation to

An ideal owner is one who trains their pet to be a 'good citizen' – obedient, good-natured and a pleasure to own.

help cover his keep until they do so. Alternatively, have a word with your trainer or vet as they may know of the ideal home for your pet, with someone who can offer your dog that which you cannot.

Canine fact

How you treat your dog in the first six months will set the scene for the rest of your time together. Getting it right from the beginning will be easier than backtracking later.

Top tip

The less you resort to punishment to get your own way, and the fewer times you get angry with your new dog, the quicker he will learn to trust you.

Should I get a second dog?

You want to get a second dog or puppy to provide your existing pet with a friend and company when you are out. This might seem like a good idea initially, but will the reality be as ideal as the concept? Before going ahead and getting another dog, ask yourself the following questions.

Checklist

✓ Is your existing dog likely to welcome a newcomer?
✓ Have you got the time to integrate the dogs?
✓ Can you cope with the inevitable routine upheaval of integration?
✓ Can you afford another dog?
✓ Have you got the space and facilities for keeping two dogs?
✓ Could you ably deal with any behaviour problems that may arise?

Compatibility

While most dogs are highly social animals, introducing a resident dog to a newcomer is not always as easy as you might imagine it to be. So, it is important to consider your existing dog's temperament before getting another one. Some breeds do not co-exist well with other dogs, so this is another consideration – see pages 12–19 for information on different breed and type characteristics.

Two dogs that get on well together enjoy a wonderful friendship – and you get twice the pleasure! If one or both are neutered, there is less need for them to be competitive.

Frequently asked question

Q I'd like to get another dog, but what will my existing dog's reaction be?

A Not all dogs adjust to a life with other dogs (see 'Compatibility' above). Watch out for signs of bullying by the stronger dog. If, after a month or so, either dog is very unhappy with the situation, or there are often fights and scuffles between them, it may be kinder to rehome the new dog.

Your dog may not welcome another on his territory – especially if your dog is of a highly territorial nature, has not been well socialized with other dogs previously, or is used to your undivided and doting attention.

Introducing a second dog

Dogs do not live by the same code of conduct that humans do, so, instead of smiling and shaking hands on first meeting, they may well swear at each other and have a punch-up. As this would not start the relationship off on the right footing, careful introductions are essential so that this situation does not occur.

Bonding

Some dogs bond so closely that the owner is left out of the equation. To avoid this happening, you will need to separate the dogs if they are left alone for any length of time, either during the day while you are at work, or at night. Do this by means of a mesh partition or a stair gate so they can still keep each other company, but can't play together unless you are there to supervise it. So that the dogs won't feel entirely 'abandoned' during the day, give them something to occupy their time alone such as activity toys, or have someone come in to give them attention, to take them for a walk, and just to let them outside to relieve themelseves. It is also a good idea regularly to take each dog out separately, so that you can devote your attention to each one singly. The new dog will learn to be confident when out alone, and not to rely on the other dog for support.

Usually, introductions between a new dog and the existing one go smoothly, with the new dog acting, and being treated like, a visitor. The hierarchy between them is normally sorted out reasonably amicably within the first few weeks.

DO

• Follow the steps given in 'Socializing' on pages 74–79 and in 'Bringing your dog home' on pages 54–57.

• Expect integration to take some time.

• Allow the dogs to investigate each other at their own pace without distractions.

• Feed the dogs separately to begin with.

• Give the new dog his own bed and toys to minimize disagreements over possessions.

• Initially, reinforce the existing dog's position as leader of the canine 'pack' by favouring him first when playing, feeding, giving attention and allowing him to go through doorways first.

DON'T

• Interfere in the natural process of the dogs sorting out the hierarchy between themselves in the first couple of weeks – unless they begin to actually fight. If it becomes obvious that the new dog has taken control, you will have to reinforce this by putting the new dog first in everything instead.

• Aggravate a situation between the dogs during the settling-in period; for example, shut them in separate rooms to fuss and give them treats.

• Lift (in the case of small dogs) one dog above the other; by doing so, you will give the underdog a height advantage that can trigger the top dog into aggression.

• Leave the dogs together until you are certain they have become friends.

CARING FOR A DOG

Part of the attraction of owning one of these wonderful creatures is the interaction many owners enjoy in keeping their dog happy and healthy. There are many aspects to dog care and management, and it is extremely satisfying to know that you are paying meticulous attention to all the needs of the animal in your care. For many people, the daily routine involved in looking after a dog, from preparing his dinner to enjoying a romp in the countryside, is very fulfilling, and the loyal and unwavering affection received in return supremely rewarding.

Handling dogs

The manner in which you handle and interact with your dog will affect his behaviour and reactions towards you. In situations where there is tension in the air, they hear loud or raised voices, they are touched roughly or they are grabbed at suddenly, dogs feel threatened and insecure. Dogs respond better to, and prefer, people who behave as shown on the checklist.

Checklist

✓ they touch the dog gently
✓ they are unhurried and deliberate in their actions
✓ they are at ease
✓ they speak in a low, soft voice
✓ they avoid eye contact

Physical communication

Most pet dogs learn to enjoy being fussed and stroked from an early age and appreciate being touched – particularly on the back, chest and sides, which are 'safe' areas. Areas that a dog will instinctively be wary about having touched are his eyes, mouth, paws, ears, tummy, tail and anal area. However, it is important to accustom your dog to having these areas touched without a fuss, in case they need grooming or veterinary attention.

Dogs threaten each other by staring and they learn quickly to take avoiding action if this happens, rather than risk the aggression that would otherwise accompany it. Humans tend to gaze lovingly at their pet, so it is important to teach your pet that staring from humans is fine.

Have you ever thought about what effect the way you physically communicate with your dog has on his mental and physical well-being? While you imagine that a good-natured thump or strong patting on your dog's rib or back, or even a boisterous 'wrestle' or ear-fondling session, signifies your affection for him, such treatment is likely to be uncomfortable or even downright painful for your pet. Try it on yourself and you'll see what I mean. Gentle stroking is the best way of indicating your love and regard for him.

Vocal communication

A dog's hearing is much more acute than ours. Loud noise, therefore, causes dogs discomfort and fear. Don't raise your voice in anger towards your dog, or subject him to blaring music or loud volume from the television. In addition, avoid sudden movements or loud noises directed at your dog, which he could construe as being aggressive. Dogs respond best to gentle, low and soothing tones – they may not understand the words that their owners are saying to them, but they do understand the meaning conveyed through the tone of voice. This applies equally when you use harsh tones.

Compared with children, dogs are less able to understand sounds used as signals and find it quite hard to learn vocal commands, such as 'sit' and 'come here'. It is much easier for them to learn such spoken commands if they are given in conjunction with hand signals or gestures during training. The hand signal can be gradually withdrawn as the dog becomes better educated.

Give him space

Dogs are quick to sense their owners' emotions, and when all is not well they can be upset. Your dog needs a space to retreat to until he senses that you are in a good mood and ready to give him attention. This 'sanctuary' is also a place where he can hide from children, or other pets in the household, when he has had enough of interaction.

Top tip

Dogs that have not been taught to accept being hugged feel threatened by such an action from a human and will try to escape, or may even bite, in response to the perceived 'attack'. It is therefore vital that children are taught not to try to hug such dogs, as the results can be tragic.

Did you know ...?

To help a timid dog feel more comfortable in your presence, turn sideways, crouch down (to make yourself smaller and therefore less threatening) and avoid eye contact. Adopting this posture can also defuse a potentially difficult situation with a nervous dog.

Picking up your dog

See page 159 for how to handle and move an injured dog.

1 *Crouch down and gently but firmly gather your dog to you, with one arm around his chest to keep him from breaking free and the other arm under his bottom for support.*

2 *While keeping the dog close to your body, so that he feels safe and secure and can't jump from your arms, stand up slowly.*

3 *Carry the dog close to your chest. To put him down, simply reverse the actions. Throughout, bend from the knees to avoid straining your back.*

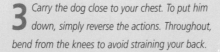

Dogs and children

According to research, children who grow up with pets in the house, and who are taught to treat them with respect and care, are more likely to do better at school and develop into well-balanced and responsible adults. If you are a parent, there can be no better reason to have a dog. To create harmony between children and a dog, follow the advice in the checklist.

Checklist

✓ supervise interaction
✓ teach children to respect the dog
✓ show children correct handling and training procedures
✓ encourage bonding
✓ involve children in daily care
✓ forbid cruelty

Safety

If there are children in the household, they must be taught to respect the dog and how to correctly handle and speak to him. It is surprising just how tolerant some dogs and puppies can be with babies and young children, but this is not something you should put to the test. You must teach children not to disturb the dog – especially by grabbing at him – when he is resting in his bed, or eating his food, or he may bite. It is advisable to steer clear of the more naturally aggressive breeds if you have children, and carefully choose one of the more gentle, equable types.

Never leave young children alone with a dog, no matter how good-natured or trustworthy you think the animal is. Often, quite unintentionally, children can harass a dog unmercifully, until he can take no more and bites to warn them off (as he would an unruly pup in the pack). This is unacceptable in a human environment so, for everyone's sake, do not put the dog or children in a situation in which they are at risk.

Interaction and playing

It is important to keep an eye on children when they are playing with a dog. They can get carried away and not realize when a game is getting out of hand, with the dog becoming overexcited and therefore liable to play rough.

Make sure that your children teach your puppy or adult dog only good behaviour. Show them what to do if the dog jumps up at them or pulls at their clothes, what to do if he play-bites, and how to tell the dog what they want and how to play acceptable games. Show them how to stroke the dog gently and where your dog appreciates being petted. Get your children to help feed the dog, and show them how to tell him to sit and wait for his meal before they allow him to have it. This is to reinforce their pack status over the dog's, and also so that the dog regards them as being rewarding

It Is important that children – and even adult visitors – know not to take liberties with your dog such as grabbing at his tail or paws in play, and not to encourage him to play-bite at arms or clothing.

and a good thing to have around because they supply him with food.

Discreetly supervising all their activities together will prevent either party learning or doing the wrong thing.

Hygiene

Children tend to put their hands in their mouths at every opportunity. Although it is rare for a child to pick up any infection (such as ringworm, tapeworm and toxocariasis) from dogs, you must take great care to ensure that children (and adults, including yourself) always wash their hands after handling a dog (and other animals too) to minimize any risk.

Toxocara canis is the parasitic worm carried by dogs and passed out in their faeces that is the cause of toxocariasis in humans. Most infections are harmless if the person concerned (expectant mothers included) has got sufficient immunity against them. Worming your dog regularly is good practice to keep the risk of contracting toxocariasis to a minimum.

Playing together is a great way of expending excess energy in both your dog and your children.

Discourage children from playing tug games with your dog, because they may not know when to stop. The dog could become reluctant to relinquish the tug, and become aggressive towards the child.

Routine care

Dogs need help from their owners to lead happy, fulfilled and healthy lives. To maintain your pet's mental and physical health, certain routine procedures must be carried out on a daily, monthly and yearly basis, shown in the checklist.

Checklist

✓ correct nutrition (food and water)
✓ grooming
✓ exercise
✓ training
✓ monitoring behaviour, body eliminations and appearance
✓ providing stimulating activities
✓ checking vital signs
✓ parasite control
✓ arranging for vaccinations

Body condition

Pet dogs can suffer from obesity if they do not get enough exercise in relation to the food they receive on a daily basis. Being overweight can seriously affect your dog's health and shorten his life. Ask the breeder or your vet what the ideal weight for your dog is so that you can keep track of any deviation from this, which may indicate a health problem.

Urine and faeces (eliminations)

The most important things to look out for are:
• discomfort in urinating and/or defecating
• unusual elimination, such as defecating/urinating in the house when normally your dog is clean
• a constant need to eliminate, often with no satisfactory result

• blood in the faeces or urine, or other abnormalities such as very loose or very hard stools
• not as many eliminations as normal
• worms in the faeces (resembling grains of rice or slim, white threads)

Any deviation in usual elimination should be closely monitored. If this persists for more than a day, seek veterinary advice. If worms are seen in the faeces, deworm your dog.

Top tip

Check your dog's collar fit regularly – especially on growing puppies – to ensure it is not too tight or too loose, and that it is not chafing. You should be able to fit two fingers between the collar and your dog's neck.

Straining to eliminate can indicate that your dog is suffering from a digestive upset. If it persists for more than a day, seek veterinary advice.

General demeanour

If you know your dog well, you will notice any difference in his behaviour and demeanour. If he is normally active and perky, but suddenly appears depressed, then it indicates he is feeling poorly. If other signs that all is not well appear, take him to the vet for a check-up. Make a note of the symptoms, so that you can fully inform the vet, which may help him or her to determine what ails your pet. See pages 28–29 for what signs to look for in a healthy and an unhealthy dog, and also pages 140–143 for routine health care.

If you know your dog well, you will soon notice from his appearance and demeanour if something is bothering him.

Check a dog's pulse rate by placing two fingers on the femoral artery found underneath the skin at the top of the dog's inner thigh, as shown. It is the quality as well as the number per minute of pulse (heart) beats that is important; a weak pulse rate can indicate a blood-circulation problem.

Canine fact

A dog's vital signs – temperature, pulse and respiration (TPR) – alter depending on his age and size, and on the weather. In hot weather, for example, his vital signs will be slightly higher than usual. Find out what your dog's usual TPR is by taking his temperature, pulse and respiration rates, when he is at rest, over a period of a week (in summer and in winter) to discover his average during warm and cold seasons. Bear in mind that the pulse and respiration rates will also be higher following exercise and when he is excited or fearful. As a guide, canine vital signs are:

• **Temperature** 38.1–38.6°C (100.5–101.5°F)
• **Pulse** 62–130 beats per minute depending on size; the smaller the dog, the more rapid the pulse
• **Respiration** 10–30 breaths per minute; smaller dogs breathe faster

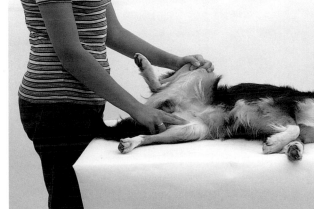

Training

Maintain the rules about what your pet is and isn't allowed to do on a daily basis, so as not to confuse him. Stick to the same vocal and physical commands. Make sure that other members of the family and visitors also abide by these rules.

Special occasion care

At times when celebrations occur, such as Christmas or New Year, dogs need extra-special care so that they do not become stressed with all the noise and extra people in the house, and/or ill through eating anything unsuitable. Festive decorations and Christmas trees can prove irresistible to curious and playful canines, so make sure that trees are well secured in their stands, lights are plugged into a circuit breaker, and that baubles are shatterproof.

Dogs love to be part of the party, and it is only right that yours should be included as a member of the family, but when you sense he is becoming overwhelmed by all the goings-on, then put him in a quieter part of the house, perhaps with an activity toy to keep him pleasantly occupied, so he can chill out and rest.

Even though you may be tempted to, don't give your dog foods he does not normally receive, such as cakes, sweets and chocolate, otherwise he may suffer unpleasant and painful tummy upsets – but, of course, you can give him his own present of a new toy and a few treats to open with the rest of the family.

Firework use during celebrations seems to be increasing. Most animals are terrified of fireworks, so if they are going off in the neighbourhood keep your dog safely indoors. Having the TV or radio on can help drown the noise. If you are planning a fireworks party, keep your dog inside, preferably in a room on the other side of the house and only buy 'silent' fireworks. Inform neighbours of a forthcoming fireworks party. An advance warning gives them the chance to take precautions against their pets becoming distressed.

Frequently asked question

Q How often should I take my dog to training class?

A Every week for puppies and juveniles is preferred until you have at least mastered the basics of obedient behaviour and good manners (see pages 106–127). Thereafter, try to go once every two weeks, and at the least once a month, to maintain good behaviour and manners and to help stop bad habits from forming in the way you address and interact with your dog. Also, it is important to spend some time every day maintaining training standards, otherwise things tend to slip and problem behaviour can start to occur. Remember – you have to put in the work to reap the rewards of a well-behaved dog.

Once your dog has mastered the basics, put some time aside to train your dog every couple of weeks.

AT-A-GLANCE MAINTENANCE CHECKS

FREQUENCY	WHAT TO DO
Daily	• Clean food and water bowls • Feed and supply fresh water • Check eating habits • Check for abnormalities in eliminations • Exercise and spend quality time together • Groom longhaired or thick-coated dogs • Check collar fit • Check for signs of injury, illness and unusual lumps and bumps • Train • Clear faeces from the garden
Weekly	• Groom shorthaired dogs • Check ears for wax or hair build-up • General check for elderly dogs – vital signs • Check food stocks for forthcoming week • Wash and disinfect water and food bowls using a pet bowl cleaner or saline solution, and rinse well • Check for weight loss or gain • Training class for puppies and juveniles • Clean teeth (see page 97)
Fortnightly	• Worm puppies for roundworm and tapeworm – first at 2 weeks of age, and then every fortnight until they are 12 weeks of age; get the wormer from your vet and ask their advice on the correct dosage for your dog • Training class to keep you and your dog 'sharp' and to help prevent or solve behaviour/obedience problems
Monthly	• Treat your dog for fleas – ask your vet which product would be most suitable; and whether it is administered monthly or three-monthly (see page 142 for detailed information on fleas and worms) • General health check, including vital signs (see 'Canine fact' page 91)
Every three months	• Worm your dog (aged 12 weeks plus) against roundworm and tapeworm; get the wormer from your vet and seek their advice on the correct dosage
Every six months	• Veterinary check-up for elderly dogs
Once a year	• Vaccination boosters (see page 143) and general veterinary check-up

Puppy care

For that appealing puppy to grow into the perfect pet, you need to put in lots of work. This will not be hard – common sense, inclination and the will to apply certain training principles and procedures into training your puppy how to behave and perform as you wish him to will do the trick nicely. The checklist gives the basics of good puppy care.

Checklist

✔ patience, kindness and gentleness
✔ understanding canine behaviour
✔ appropriate veterinary attention
✔ consistent training
✔ setting rules and abiding by them
✔ correct handling
✔ spending quality time together
✔ rewarding and promoting appropriate behaviour

Handling, interaction and socializing

Establishing yourselves as higher in rank than your puppy is one of the most important and kindest things you and your family can do for him as he grows into adolescence and adulthood. By firmly establishing his place at the bottom of the pack, you are helping to ensure he has a much better quality of life when he grows up than a puppy that has been allowed to run riot and have all his own way.

See pages 86–87 for how to handle dogs, pages 88–89 for how to integrate dogs and children, and pages 74–79 for information on training and socializing.

Playing correctly with your puppy will help you form a strong bond with him, provide him with essential exercise and also lay the groundwork for behaviour and obedience training (for example, rolling a ball for him to chase can be developed into 'fetch, recall and give' exercises). Therefore play is ultimately vital for your puppy's mental and physical well-being.

Birth to rehoming

For information on caring for puppies from birth to rehoming, see pages 150–155.

Feeding

If you get your puppy from a rescue centre or reputable breeder, ask for a diet sheet, detailing the food type, how much of it and how many meals a day he is receiving. Carry on with this, being sure to follow the life-stage feeding guides on page 44 as your puppy matures, to meet his nutritional needs.

Playing

After eating and sleeping, play comes high in a puppy's priorities; indeed, this is essential for his development. He will amuse himself for ages with an assortment of toys (an old sock knotted in the middle provides a cheap but highly enjoyable plaything) and, of course, his human playmates. Toys must be suitable for puppies, and you should replace them if they

become dangerously damaged, so that the pup does not swallow torn-off pieces that may cause serious digestive disturbances or blockages.

The more games you play with your puppy, the more he will consider you to be the most interesting thing in the world. The more he wants to be with you and please you, the easier he will be to control. Such dogs are much more fun to have around and are more sociable.

Praise and reward

Dogs love being praised and rewarded, and soon learn which types of behaviour reap good things; they will therefore strive to attain these from you. Learning which acts gain praise and reward, and noting those that don't is a vital part of a dog's education – and forms the basis of the quickest and most pleasant way to train him.

Discipline

Only rarely should you need to correct your puppy. Most of your interactions should be happy and pleasant, which will mean you become a good friend and your puppy will try hard to please you. Manipulate situations so that he does the right thing and can be rewarded for doing so, rather than allowing him to do something you don't like and then telling him off for it.

If discipline is necessary, give it in a similar way to how a bitch would discipline her pups. It should be immediate, startling, effective and over in seconds. Then show him the correct behaviour and reward him for doing it. If he is about to do something unacceptable, warn him not to first. Do this by saying 'No!', 'Arghhh', or something similar, in a deep, stern and growly voice.

If he continues with what he is doing, then follow the warning

Top tip

Keep games short and fun and end on a good note so they represent a positive experience for your puppy. Never get angry or impatient with him while playing together, or it will put him off playing positively, which will in turn hamper training progress as well as encourage undesirable behaviour.

If you don't want your puppy to chew things that belong to you, don't encourage him to play with such items or he will, naturally, view them as fair game.

immediately with a correction – before he carries out the unwanted behaviour, such as chomping on your

Did you know ...?

Generally, smacking your dog is wrong. Not only can it cause resentment and a fear of humans, but it very often sows the seeds of aggression towards them. Physically punishing your dog means you lack self-discipline and are too lazy to learn correct disciplinary techniques.

leg. Surprise him by shouting, growling or clapping loudly at him, thus preventing the intended behaviour. Tower over and stare at him, until he backs off. You may have to push him away at the same time if he persists. Then show him that the correct way to behave is more rewarding. For example, if he sits quietly, revert to being calm and pleasant and reward him.

It is important to tailor the level of the correction needed to your puppy – some are more sensitive than others. If, after a correction, your puppy appears sulky and wary of you, you are overcorrecting; if he carries on doing the things you have previously corrected, you are undercorrecting.

Get your puppy used to being handled by lots of people – this is an important part of his socialization process.

Handling and grooming

Your puppy needs to learn to be groomed, hugged, touched and restrained on your terms. The more puppies are familiarized with these procedures, the less they feel threatened by such experiences and the less likely they are to bite when touched, particularly during stressful situations such as visiting the vet. Touching and stroking the puppy all over, as well as holding, gently hugging and restraining him, builds a trust and an acceptance that will be

Too much exercise or play can damage soft, growing bones and joints in dogs of all sizes, leading to health problems later.

projected on to people outside the immediate family.

Start grooming sessions as soon as you get your puppy. Keep them short to begin with, gradually extending the time taken to groom him. See pages 98–101 for more information on grooming, and pages 86–87 for more information on general handling procedures.

Oral hygiene

As soon as you get your puppy, get him used to having his mouth opened and inspected, and also to having his teeth cleaned to help prevent tartar build-up and periodontal disease (see page 165). To clean his teeth, start by rubbing your finger dipped in dog toothpaste on his gums and teeth. Once he is used to this, progress to using a dog toothbrush, or finger tooth-glove, and gently brush his gums and teeth. Both the toothbrushes and toothpaste are available from pet stores.

Vaccinations

For many reasons, some people are for vaccinating dogs, while others are against (the frequency of booster jabs being a particular problem). However – from the veterinary point of view and due to a lack of scientific evidence to prove otherwise – the balance is in favour of vaccination

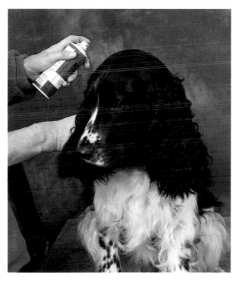

because there are some unpleasant and lethal diseases that dogs can fall victim to.

Some insurance companies insist that dogs are vaccinated before they will issue policies; if vaccinations are not kept up to date, the insurers may not pay out in the event of a claim, so check the terms before signing up. See page 57 and page 143 for further information on vaccination.

Canine fact

Between the ages of 12 weeks and 6 months, your puppy will shed his milk teeth. These are replaced by permanent (adult) teeth.

Consult your vet regarding flea control for puppies aged up to 6 months – there are several effective products available from vets, comprising spot-on, spray and tablet treatments, but the strength of the one used depends on the type and weight of the young dog. See page 142 for further information on flea control.

Frequently asked question

Q When should I treat my new puppy for worms?

A Roundworms and tapeworms can cause all sorts of health problems, even death, so consult your vet regarding a suitable worming product and programme for your puppy. A typical regime is to worm puppies at 2 weeks, then fortnightly until 12 weeks, and thereafter every 3 months. See page 142 for more information on worms and deworming, and page 89 for details on toxocariasis.

Grooming

Grooming is an essential aspect of owning a dog. It will help you bond with him, and check for any unusual lumps and bumps, as well as keeping his coat and skin in good condition. The right tools for the job will depend on your dog's coat type; you will need some or all of the items on the checklist.

Did you know ...?

Depending on your dog's size, it is usually easier to groom him on a table. Never leave him unattended on one, however.

Checklist

- ✓ grooming glove
- ✓ old towels (or similar)
- ✓ silky or velvet cloth or duster
- ✓ guillotine-type nail-clippers
- ✓ round-edged scissors
- ✓ straight scissors
- ✓ tweezers
- ✓ cotton wool
- ✓ ear, eye and undertail wipes
- ✓ dry or wet shampoo
- ✓ spray-on conditioner
- ✓ wash-in conditioner
- ✓ hairclips (for longhaired dogs)
- ✓ tearstain remover
- ✓ toothbrush and toothpaste for dogs
- ✓ trimming comb and blades
- ✓ electric clippers and blades
- ✓ de-matting tool
- ✓ forceps (for inner ear hair removal)
- ✓ bristle brush
- ✓ slicker brush (not suitable for thin-coated dogs)
- ✓ rubber brush or slicker (ideal for thin-coated dogs)
- ✓ rubber bath mat
- ✓ non-slip cloth/mat for table
- ✓ baby talcum powder/ grooming powder
- ✓ box to put the grooming gear in
- ✓ fine-toothed (flea) comb
- ✓ wide-toothed comb
- ✓ stripping stone
- ✓ stripping knife
- ✓ thinning scissors
- ✓ anti-static spray
- ✓ coat shedder
- ✓ friends

Frequently asked question

Q How often should I bathe my dog, and how should I go about doing this?

A A bath every 2–3 months or so is adequate for most dogs. Don't wash your pet more often than this unless really necessary, or you will strip the natural oils from the coat, making it dry and frizzy unless you take steps to prevent this by applying coat conditioners.

Groom your dog thoroughly before bathing. Wash him in the bath or the kitchen sink (put a plug sieve in to trap hairs when you let the water out, so as not to clog the drain), or outside in a suitably sized tub – whichever method is most practical. The water temperature should be tepid. Wet the dog thoroughly, then apply dog shampoo, working it well into the coat to make a good lather. Rinse it all out with tepid water, shampoo again if the dog is very greasy, rinse, and then apply conditioner. Some conditioners can be left in the coat, others need to be rinsed out.

Dry the dog off with a towel, then groom the coat through to remove knots. Use a hair-dryer and brush to blow-dry the coat (keep your hand in the airflow to ensure the air is not too hot), or leave the dog to dry naturally if the weather is warm and dry. Take care not to get water, shampoo or conditioner in the dog's ears and eyes.

Why groom?

As well as to improve appearance and help keep him healthy, your dog needs grooming to:

• keep shed hair around the house to a minimum

• remove dead hair and prevent the coat from knotting and matting (felting) in longhaired, curly-coated and double-coated dogs

• check for fleas, mites and skin ailments

• make him easier to handle

• make your pet feel good as regards his appearance

• ensure he is happy to have all areas of his body attended to

• help your pet feel more comfortable, relaxed, pampered, and generally better within himself

Canine fact

A dog's 'armpits' can get very knotted in longhaired breeds, so you must pay attention to these areas. Using hairclips to separate lengths of hair on the body and head as you are grooming these areas can make the job easier.

COAT TYPES

TYPE	EXAMPLES	REQUIREMENTS
Wire-haired	• Airedale • Parson Jack Russell Terrier • Border Terrier	These coats need to be brushed daily, and hand-stripped to maintain their shape and appearance three or four times a year; the latter is best done by a professional groomer.
Double	• Old English Sheepdog • German Shepherd Dog • Cross-breeds • Newfoundland • Rough Collie • Golden Retriever	Daily attention is required for some double coats (dense top and undercoats), such as the Old English Sheepdog (it can take up to an hour to groom properly daily), while others with less dense top coats, such as the German Shepherd Dog, are usually fine with a weekly thorough brushing. Some breeds, such as the Old English Sheepdog, Samoyed and Chow Chow, benefit from professional grooming every two months or so.
Smooth	• Cross-breeds • Rhodesian Ridgeback • Labrador Retriever • Rottweiler • Dobermann	A weekly groom should suffice, but you may have to brush your pet more often than this if he has a dense undercoat, such as in the Labrador Retriever.
Long	• Afghan Hound • Spaniels • Setters • Shih Tzu	Daily grooming is required to remove dead hair and knots. If professionally groomed for the best results, this should be done every six weeks, on top of your daily brushing.
Curly/woolly	• Bichon Frise • Poodles • Bedlington Terrier	Curly coats do not moult, but shed hair within the existing coat. Such breeds need regular grooming every other day to remove dead hair, plus professional clipping every six weeks or so to maintain coat shape and style.

How to groom

The method used very much depends on the coat type, and it is wise to ask the breeder to show you how to maintain your dog's coat if he has a high-maintenance coat type. If nails need clipping and hairy inner ears need attention, then again ask the breeder to show you what to do. Otherwise, leave coat trimming and shaping to the professional groomer, unless you intend to learn how to clip, strip and/or trim it yourself.

Maintain the coat by brushing or combing out dead hair on a daily or weekly basis, as required. The tools you use will depend on the coat type and density of undercoat. The steps to follow are as follows.

• Remove dead undercoat – getting right down to the skin, but taking care not to snag or pull it – and tease out knots.

• Brush or comb through the top coat and remove further loose hair.

• Massage a conditioning (protein) finishing spray into the coat to give it a sheen, and remove more dead hair.

• Wipe the eyes, inner ears if necessary and under the tail to freshen your pet up. Never poke down the ears with cotton buds, as you risk damaging the delicate structure inside.

Moulting

Shedding of hair in a seasonal pattern is normal in most breeds, but central heating seems to have interfered with the pattern in many dogs, resulting in them shedding hair all year round. Apart from regular grooming, there is little you can do to prevent such shedding apart from perhaps turning the heating down.

1 To begin grooming, put one hand around the dog's chest and shoulders to steady him, and prevent him jumping off the table, if he is on one.

2 Brush the back of the neck, down the back and the sides first, then between the hind legs and under the tummy – taking care not to snag the genitals and nipples with brush or comb teeth, nor to knock bony protuberances with the brush. When brushing, imagine you are brushing your own hair – your dog will soon tell you if you are being too firm or rough.

3 Brush the legs and head last. Be gentle with the head, talking comfortingly to your pet and praising him if he doesn't make a fuss. If he plays up and you are sure this isn't because you are brushing too hard or causing him discomfort, be firm and insist that he stays put to be groomed until you have finished.

Handling practice

Getting your dog used to having his ears, eyes and mouth handled from the start will make grooming him easier. Routinely check inside his ears, wipe his eyes with dampened cotton wool or eye wipes, and lift his lips to inspect and touch his teeth (see page 97 for how to clean teeth). Give him lots of praise during the handling when he allows you to inspect these areas without fuss, so that he views you doing so as a rewarding experience.

Top tip

Never bath a dog with a matted coat – it will just make the mats worse and harder to groom out. Tease the knots out gently first with a comb and/or de-matting tool, taking care not to pull at the skin, then brush the coat out thoroughly, and only then bath the dog. In bad cases of matting, the only – and kindest – solution is to clip off the coat completely.

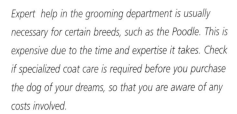

Expert help in the grooming department is usually necessary for certain breeds, such as the Poodle. This is expensive due to the time and expertise it takes. Check if specialized coat care is required before you purchase the dog of your dreams, so that you are aware of any costs involved.

Dogs and travel

For every owner, there are times when you have to be away from home – for holidays, visiting friends and family, hospitalization or business trips, for example. During such times, you will have to make arrangements for your dog to be looked after. There are several options to choose from (see the checklist), depending on the circumstances.

Checklist

✓ boarding kennels
✓ family, friends and neighbours
✓ petsitter
✓ taking the dog with you

Take your dog's favourite toy and his bed and/or bedding so he has something familiar to help him settle in boarding kennels.

Did you know ...?

If your dog is or looks unwell when presented at a boarding kennels, it is within their right to refuse him entry, as he may pose a risk to other dogs there.

Boarding kennels

Seek recommendations from vets and dog-owning friends. Visit likely establishments first to satisfy yourself your dog will be well cared for. Your dog will need to be vaccinated against relevant diseases, so ensure his inoculations are up to date well in advance (see page 143). Take the vaccination certificate with you when presenting your pet at kennels as it will be checked. Tell the kennels of any special care your dog needs, or if he has any behaviour problems.

Petsitters

If you have a number of pets, employing the services of a petsitter is a good option. Such a person stays in your house, so you have the added advantage of home security as well as your pets being cared for in familiar surroundings. Use a reputable agency that vets its staff carefully, and offers insurance in case of mishaps.

Leave the following information for pet carers before you depart:
• contact details for yourself and your vet, in case they need to contact you or the vet in an emergency
• what food your dog has, how much and when; leave enough food for the entire period of your absence
• any medical details if your dog is receiving treatment
• any specific dos and don'ts regarding your pet's care and handling
• maps and duration times of safe, local walks if required

Taking your dog on holiday with you

If you want to take your dog away with you, you need to accustom him to travelling. If using public transport, check companies' rules and regulations regarding this. In the car, travelling your dog in a travel crate is the safest option – make sure that he can stand up, lie down and turn around in it. Incorporate plenty of rest and stops in the journey, and never leave your dog unattended in the car – particularly on warm days (see page 170).

Taking your dog abroad

These days, taking your dog abroad is much easier, thanks to the introduction of the Pet Travel Scheme (PETS). As this scheme is a relatively new ruling, the conditions change fairly frequently, so you need to find out from the relevant government department which vaccinations, ID requirements and parasite treatment are needed for your dog to leave and re-enter your country. Make sure you have the appropriate documentation, that your pet has been vaccinated and parasite-treated within specified times, and that he has the approved ID microchip, to avoid confusion when entering and leaving countries.

Check out and book pet-friendly accommodation in the area you intend to visit with your dog well in advance, and ask what rules and regulations they impose on pet guests to ensure you are able to comply with them.

Frequently asked question

Q I'd like to take my pet on holiday in my own country. Is this a good idea?

A Many hotels are pet-friendly these days. Dogs are generally contented to be where their owners are, and are always more than happy to explore new places and walks, so both of you are likely to enjoy going away on holiday together. Take your dog's bed, toys, food, collar and leash, and a first-aid kit so you are prepared for any eventuality. Find out where the nearest vet is in the area. Make sure your dog is wearing an ID tag bearing your holiday address and phone number as well as your permanent one, in case he gets lost while away. Having him ID microchipped is a good idea.

Canine fact

One of the easiest ways to acquaint yourself with PETS rules and regulations is to check your country's rules via the internet – simply key in 'pet travel abroad' to a good search engine. Alternatively, contact your local environmental agency or veterinary clinic. Use only relevant government-approved or licensed vets to ensure your dog receives the appropriate treatment and certification.

TRAINING YOUR DOG

Although dogs should not be attributed with having human characteristics, they are intelligent enough to be able to grasp the concept of, and execute, certain actions that their owners require of them – if these actions are requested in a way that dogs find rewarding. So, with this principle in mind, owners have to be clever too and find a way of training their dog that works quickly and effectively. This section explains how to achieve this ideal – how to speak 'dog' so that you are able to communicate effectively with your four-legged friend.

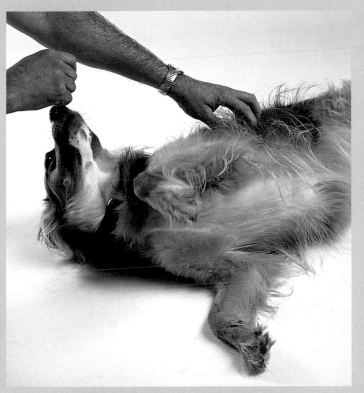

Why training is essential

Frankly, an untrained dog can be a real nuisance – a hazard to himself, his owner and to other people and animals. Owning an undisciplined pet can result in any of the problems on the checklist.

Having a well-trained dog makes looking after him easier and much more pleasurable, and he is likely to get a much better reaction from people throughout his life. So you owe it to your pet to train him correctly and well.

Safety

Not only can it be extremely inconvenient to own an untrained and disobedient dog, but it can also severely affect your health (and that of third parties), social status and finances, and often results in the dog being rehomed, or even abandoned, through no fault of his own.

Common injuries suffered by dog owners are those sustained in the home or out on walks due to their dog barging into them, pulling them along, or being aggressive. Third-party injuries result from people being injured as a result of off-lead dogs ignoring their owners' recall commands and attacking or chasing them, and also through dogs running on to roads and causing traffic accidents. This leads to claims by those third parties pursuing dog owners for injuries and/or damages caused.

Not only does an untrained dog put humans, and indeed other animals, at risk, but he is at risk of injury and even

Canine fact

Dogs that always get their own way will think that life revolves around them and therefore they must be important. Since dogs are looking at controlling different resources than humans, their bid for power often goes unnoticed until it is too late. Obedience-training your dog and ensuring he is not elevated to a top position within the home will keep your relationship with him well balanced in your favour – as it should be for contentment all round.

If you get a puppy, you will need to be prepared to spend a good deal of time house-training him and establishing basic obedience.

Top tip

You must put the work into training your dog to achieve the results you want.

death himself – either from injuries sustained while out of control, or because of being destroyed due to his owners being unable to cope with him and no one else being willing to adopt a canine delinquent.

Good manners

Some people who own untrained, and therefore badly behaved, dogs cannot understand why their circle of friends decreases and no one seems to want to visit them any more. They fail to appreciate that most visitors do not like being jumped all over and covered with hairs and slobber!

Having a dog that will obey the basics of obedience-training – he walks to heel, obeys recall and goes and lies down out of the way on command – makes for an easier and more pleasurable life for all concerned. If you are continually telling the dog off for doing something you consider to be inappropriate, but not teaching him clearly and kindly the right way to go about things, this leads to a very stressful existence for you both – which is unpleasant and not good for either party's health.

Successful relationships are based on positive two-way communication and respect. If you want your dog to be well behaved with impeccable manners then you will find that understanding how he thinks will help you attain this goal and therefore be able to establish a more mutually rewarding partnership with him.

Did you know ...?

People are bitten more often on the hands than anywhere else on their body. From the dog's point of view, hands coming towards him can appear quite frightening, especially if he had an unpleasant experience associated with them in the past. To help prevent accidents, it is essential to teach your dog that hands do not represent a threat, and also when out walking your dog to warn strangers – especially children who tend to be drawn to dogs and want to pet them – not to approach and stroke him without first asking your permission to do so.

A bright future

Training your dog to be amenable with people and obedient to their commands will benefit your dog in more ways than you can imagine. Not only will he then be a dog that virtually everyone will love and want to own, but he himself will be more mentally comfortable living in the world of humans. Handling and training your dog correctly from puppyhood helps to stop behavioural problems developing, and retraining an adult dog can often correct those that already exist.

The right start

In only a short time, you will be amazed at how much you can achieve in training your dog to respond to your directions and behave as you wish, providing you address it correctly. Don't aim to do everything at once, especially if there is more than one area or problem to deal with. Follow the advice on the checklist.

Checklist

✓ learn how a dog thinks and feels (see pages 60–63)
✓ have the right equipment
✓ keep training sessions short and fun
✓ maintain a progress diary
✓ seek professional help when necessary
✓ adopt 'train brain' (see below)
✓ reward desirable behaviour
✓ don't reward inappropriate behaviour
✓ never lose your temper with your dog

Commands and rewards

Successful training is based upon a simple principle – reward. Generally, dogs love to please their owners, and enjoy doing so even more when they are rewarded for it. Reward-based training is, therefore, the key to attaining a happy and obedient dog. Rewarding every desired

behaviour for a particular word combined with an action will evoke a learned response. Eventually, that response will become automatic every time you say the command or display the action (just like you would automatically check your wristwatch if someone asked you the time).

Food is an all-important aspect of canine life, and therefore food rewards are likely to get the desired behaviour results you require. Food-training (i.e. teaching your dog to sit, stay and wait before he is given his food, and to leave it until he is given permission to eat) marks a good start to achieving obedience in all other areas of behaviour.

Using 'train brain'

• Be consistent in your commands and actions. Stick to the same words for commands, such as 'lie', 'down', 'sit', 'stay', 'fetch' and 'give'. Changing commands will confuse your dog. Stick with them, even if they take time to sink in. Make sure that other family members also use those commands and actions and follow your instigated code of behaviour for the dog.
• Reward desired behaviour with food, a toy or attention, and your dog will learn fast.
• Vocal commands should be encouraging and kept at an even pitch.
• Keep commands clear and well spaced out – certainly at first – so as not to confuse your dog.
• If your dog has learnt to ignore a command, and thinks it means something else – such as when you say 'heel' and he is

Keep some desirable toys – such as tugs, squeakies, activity toys and bouncy balls – aside (so that they have increased value to the dog) for special rewards. When training, give your dog one of these toys (his favourite) for performing a required action, let him play with it for a few minutes, then take it away again so it doesn't become 'ordinary'. He will soon learn that such an action or command wins a prize worth having and will be keen to respond in the required way.

Most dogs will do anything for a tasty treat. Identify which treats your pet loves and you are on to a winner. Some dogs adore fresh fruit and vegetables, such as dessert apples, greens and tender young carrots, while all are usually partial to sliced hot dog sausage and cooked liver pieces. Some commercially produced treats are also very popular.

Top tips

• Learn how to food-train correctly, and then how to employ this principle as a fast and effective route to gaining a well-behaved dog.

• If you use treats to reward while training, make sure you have a supply in your pocket (or bumbag) and that they are chopped up into tiny pieces – otherwise your dog will get very fat very quickly.

• At first, until your dog displays a learned response, reward every desired response to your commands. Thereafter, reward at random, to keep his response levels high.

• Beware of unconsciously rewarding undesirable behaviour, or your dog will assume that his inappropriate actions are acceptable. For example, don't let him push through a door in front of you, but make him wait; if you let him through unchecked, the fact that he has gone out as he desired is rewarding him.

• When training your dog, he will learn to associate a word with an action. So you must be very aware of what your body is telling him, as well as your voice. For example, if you are vocally trying to encourage the dog to come to you, ensure your body language is as welcoming as your tone of voice.

walking ahead of you and pulling, therefore he associates 'heel' with pulling – then change it for another word when you begin retraining (in this case, you could use 'side').

• Never raise your voice in anger – this is counterproductive.

• Make sure everyone who comes in contact with the dog follows your rules for him. If you don't allow him on the furniture, no one else should either; otherwise you will end up with a bewildered pet.

All dogs are different

Some dogs learn things faster than others. Large breeds tend to mature more slowly, so you sometimes need to be extra patient with them. Small dogs, on the other hand, can be too clever for their own good and you will have to be on your toes. Bear in mind that working breeds, while intelligent, have an inbred instinct to chase and retrieve, guard or herd, or all three, and require disciplined handling and training to get the very best from them. Such dogs tend to thrive on agility training and training 'tasks', such as retrieving items for you or scent-tracking items. Making training a 'game' is the key to success in all cases.

How long should training sessions last?

Doing too much in one session will overtax the dog both mentally and physically, and he will end up thoroughly confused. Aim to do one exercise – interspersed with play sessions for light relief – until you have perfected it; then move on to the next task. Keep daily training sessions short and fun: 10–15 minutes of concentrated training per hour is the maximum most dogs can cope with. Puppies do not have a prolonged attention span. Three 10-minute training sessions a day are better than one 30-minute session. Always finish on a good note, so that both you and your dog will justifiably feel pleased with, and good about, yourselves.

Keep a diary, so that you can see how progress is going, and note down areas of particular achievement or difficulty, so that you can work on those exercises that your dog finds trickier than others. Above all, stay calm, be patient and make training fun.

Finding a good trainer will be invaluable in helping you to turn your dog into a well-mannered and controllable companion. A regular training session will help point you in the right direction, as well as be a whole lot of fun. Additional on-the-spot help and advice can't be beaten when it comes to putting into practice what you have learnt on paper. Many trainers will also give you and your dog the chance to try your paws at various activities such as agility, flyball, scenting work and the increasingly popular heelwork to music.

DIY training treats

These meaty little nibbles are the perfect training treats – your dog'll do anything for one.

375 g (12 oz) ox or lambs' liver
1.5 litres (2½ pints) cold water

1 Pre-heat the oven to 140°C (275°F). Grease a baking pan or use a nonstick one.
2 Put the liver in the pan with the water, bring to the boil and simmer until cooked through (about 30 minutes).
3 Drain the water into a plastic jug and save it in the refrigerator to add to regular mixer feeds.
4 Allow the liver to cool, then cut into 1 cm (½ inch) pieces. Place the pieces in the baking pan and cook in the bottom of the oven for 1 hour.
5 Allow to cool, then serve as required. Store in the refrigerator and use within three days.

How long does it take to train a dog?

There are no set time limits to how long it should take to fully train a dog. In fact, setting time limits can be counter-productive if the owner thinks his dog is not progressing as it should. The time it takes to achieve success depends on the aptitude of both owner and dog. Continual training and reinforcement of lessons are what are most effective. This means, for example, that once you have taught your dog to, say, sit, then repeat the lesson often and reward him appropriately so that he does not forget how to respond correctly to commands and directions. Reinforcing lessons learnt on a daily basis help to keep you and your dog 'sharp', and ensures that your dog remains well mannered.

Reinforcement helps prevent bad habits forming. For example, if you allow your dog to push past you when you open a door, he will think it is alright for him to do so the next time – and the next. Similarly, if you let your dog jump around excitedly whenever he sees you get his leash out ready for 'walkies', then he will think that this is acceptable behaviour.

Frequently asked question

Q What equipment do I need for training a dog?

A Buying suitable equipment from the start helps make the job of training your dog easier. You would be surprised at what a difference it makes having the correct length of leash for your particular size of dog.

Choose a 'kind' collar such as a half-check (shown here) or a broad collar in leather or nylon, with the weight and width appropriate for the size of the adult dog or puppy. When fitted, you should be able to get two or three fingers under it: too loose and it may slip off, too tight and it will cause discomfort – especially when your pet is eating or drinking.

Leash type is important. First, it must be comfortable for you to hold; second, it must be of suitable length to maintain a slack tension – if too short your pet will be dragged along, too long and you will have metres of leash to cope with. Choose a nylon leash that can be extended or shortened as desired, and then you have the best of both worlds. For artificial training aids, see page 32.

Canine fact

A training progress diary is an invaluable reference. It can also help a dog trainer and/or canine behaviourist assess you both should you need their help.

Training a puppy

A responsible and caring owner will want to guide and train their new puppy into maturing into a well-mannered adult that they can be proud of, and one that everyone will admire, love and want to own. Correctly handling and training a dog from puppyhood helps avoid behaviour problems. Your puppy needs to be able to do everything on the checklist.

Checklist

- ✓ recognize and answer to his name
- ✓ recognize and obey commands instantly
- ✓ accept sights and sounds in the environment
- ✓ be well-mannered and sociable
- ✓ be tolerant and amenable towards other people and animals
- ✓ be clean in the house
- ✓ accept being in a crate
- ✓ walk happily and obediently on a leash
- ✓ travel calmly in a vehicle

Collar and lead-training

Initially, put a collar on the puppy for short periods of time, with much praise as you do so, then distract him with a game or treat so he gets used to the feel of something around his neck and associates it with a pleasant experience. Once he is quite unconcerned by it, clip on a short lead and allow the puppy to follow you around the house, again for short periods, so he gets used to this extra attachment. Again praise and reward him fulsomely.

Once he is completely happy with his collar and lead on, you can start to teach him to walk by your side while you are holding the lead. Initially when lead-training, keep a reward (toy or treat) in your left hand so that if the puppy becomes distracted, starts pulling or lags behind you can entice him back to the correct position and pace and then reward him.

Crouch down low and call the puppy towards you. When he comes, give him a food treat and lavish praise on him – he will soon learn that coming to you when called is well rewarded.

An easy way to leash train is to hold the lead in your right hand and a reward in your left (a tasty and smelly treat or a favourite toy). Get the puppy interested in the reward. Then walk backwards and call the pup's name, keeping the lead slack and enticing him to follow you with the reward. If he is reluctant to follow, let him mouth the toy, or give him a taste of the treat, call his name again and continue backing away from him – he is sure to follow you.

Top tips

- Make training a game, so the puppy will think it is fun and not a chore or punishment.
- Check collar fit regularly as the puppy grows.

Play-training

Where any play interaction is concerned, try to channel games into what will become recall and retrieve exercises at a later stage. If the puppy brings a toy to you and drops it or gives it to you, reward this behaviour. If he relieves himself outside, praise and reward him. If he lies down beside you without pestering for attention, reward him. Use toys to gain his attention – he wants the toy, but will have to work for them.

Puppy-training classes

The best way to socialize your puppy is to take him to puppy-training classes held in a secure area, where he will be introduced to other puppies of his own age and size, as well as to other people. Allowed to intermingle together the puppies will quickly find an acceptable level of chase and play. A good trainer will ensure that play-fighting doesn't get out of hand, and that no bullying takes place and no puppy is made to feel intimidated.

Did you know ...?

A tight leash will encourage your puppy to pull against or resist it. When collar- and lead-training, walk the puppy on your left side, with a relaxed tension.

Make training a game and your puppy will respond wonderfully.

Crate-training

Training your puppy to use a crate happily will come in very handy (see page 35). However, it is important to introduce your puppy correctly to a crate, otherwise it could be viewed as a prison rather than a pleasant and safe place to be. To start with, use toys and treats to encourage your puppy to go inside it, leaving the door open so he can go in as and when he wants. Put the crate in a quiet, but not isolated, area of the house, so the puppy won't be disturbed while he is in there, but at the same time won't feel abandoned.

Take care not to place it in direct sunlight, or in areas that get too hot or cold.

Introducing the crate

• Putting comfy, familiar bedding and his favourite toys in the crate will encourage a pup to go in it and feel at home. The best time to do this initially is after a play session when he is ready for a rest.
• Accustom the pup to going in and staying in the crate by feeding him in there, at first with the door open so he doesn't feel trapped. Once he is used to this, and willingly goes in at mealtimes, feed with the door closed

Help the puppy learn that the crate is a nice place to be by giving him an activity toy filled with treats to keep him pleasurably occupied in there.

for short periods, and gradually extend these. Remember, though, that puppies generally need to relieve themselves after they have eaten.
• Gradually increase the period of time for which the puppy is left in the crate while you are at home, from a few minutes up to half an hour.
• A crate can be a great tool for toilet-training, but remember that you should only leave the puppy in it after he has eaten and then been outside. Otherwise he may need to urinate or defecate in the crate. Since dogs dislike soiling in or near their beds, having to relieve himself in the crate

could make your puppy unwilling to stay inside it.

Toilet-training

Puppies need to be taught appropriate toilet habits; they don't do this naturally. You must expect a few accidents initially, so keep him in an area where it doesn't matter if he deposits the occasional pile or puddle. Be prepared at first to take your puppy for lots of outside visits at the appropriate times, usually after eating, after playing and when he wakes up.
• Define a designated area in the garden with a length of rope. Leaving his last dropping there will indicate to him by sight and smell that this is the right place to go.
• Take your puppy there at the appropriate times and wait until he relieves himself. When he does relieve himself, praise and reward him.

Top tips

• A crate is not a 'punishment pen' and should never be used as such.
• To give the puppy extra privacy, or to encourage him to quieten down at night (providing he is not crying to show that he needs to relieve himself), cover the crate with a blanket so that he can't see out and no one can see in.
• Once used to a crate, puppies that are prone to chewing furniture, carpets and other inappropriate objects can be kept away from them until such behaviour has been cured.

Frequently asked question

Q My puppy jumps up for attention and also play-bites. Is it all right to let him do this? If not, how can I stop it?

A Unchecked, jumping up and play-biting often become more and more severe, until the dog is of a size and age where both actions really hurt and frighten human 'targets', especially children. Your puppy must be taught that both habits are unacceptable. To cure play-biting, spray a non-toxic, bitter-tasting liquid (which can be bought from pet stores) on to the area of your body that the pup normally tries to bite (usually the hands and arms). Hold out your hand and let the puppy mouth it. He will usually recoil in disgust at the foul taste and, after a number of repetitions, learn that biting humans is unpleasant. Also follow these rules.

• Make sure members of the family don't encourage the puppy to play-bite. Instead, give him toys that he can chew and play with without harming anyone.

• Handle your puppy's mouth from day one, so that he becomes accustomed to hands being in and around his jaws without biting. Praise him for letting you do this, so he learns that he is rewarded for not biting. Don't tap the pup's nose when he bites, as this will merely encourage him to do it even more.

• Don't respond to your puppy when he jumps up. Ignore him, keep your arms folded and avoid eye contact. When he gets down and makes no further attempt to jump up, reward him. This teaches the puppy that jumping up is a negative experience, whereas not doing so is a positive one.

• Most people, especially children, love to say hello to puppies (and to adult dogs) when out walking, but it is important that you ask them to refrain from doing so until the puppy sits and waits quietly for attention.

• Remember to give your puppy attention only when you have first called him to you. When you have finished fussing him, say 'enough' and gently push him away, fold your arms, avoid eye contact and ignore him.

• Make sure house visitors know and follow your rules on giving the puppy attention and what to do if he attempts to jump up at them.

When the puppy relieves himself outside, praise him so he knows that his actions, particularly if in a designated place, were desirable.

Food-training

You need to teach your puppy that it is not necessary to fight for food and that a human near his food bowl does not constitute a threat to his meal. You must also assert yourself as pack leader so the puppy eats only how and when you dictate.

• Have your puppy on a leash and put down his food bowl. Do not allow him to eat, using the leash to restrain him as necessary, along with the command 'leave'. Encourage him to remain quietly by your side, using the command 'stay' with this action.

• Wait until your puppy looks at you for permission to eat, although this may take a while. Eventually he will look to you to see whether you are ready to let him eat. When he does, say 'eat' and allow him to do so. Praise him for his patience.

• Repeat this procedure at every mealtime until your puppy will wait off-leash until he is told to eat. This training method will also enable you to teach the puppy to leave things alone and to stay and wait where you want him.

Training juvenile and adult dogs

The key to owning a well-trained dog is to start off on the right track when he is a puppy (see pages 112–115). If you have an adult dog, however, who has not been trained or whose manners leave something to be desired, then he needs to be taught the basic areas of obedience given in the checklist. This section explains how you can train your adult dog in the basics of good manners, from walking to heel on the leash to sitting, staying and behaving well in the house. Some people take these things for granted, expecting a dog to know what is required of him, but that isn't the case. He has to get to know your way of doing things, while you have to get to know him and what makes him tick.

Checklist

- ✓ leash manners
- ✓ recall
- ✓ sit and stay
- ✓ down and roll over
- ✓ road safety
- ✓ retrieve
- ✓ social skills
- ✓ house manners

Leash manners

These are important: walking a dog should be a pleasurable experience, not one you dread because the dog pulls you along, or because he dawdles sniffing every post along the way.

At first use the word 'heel' only when your dog is in the required position so he learns the word by association. Reinforce the command with a treat or praise so he learns this position is a pleasant one in which to

1 Begin with the dog on your left side, with his shoulder against your left leg and the leash held in your right hand as shown. Say your dog's name to get his attention, then 'heel'.

2 If your dog walks in front of you or pulls, stop. He will no doubt look back in surprise.

3 Get him back into position and get his attention again as in step 1. Begin walking again. Patiently repeat as required, and your pet will soon get the idea.

remain. Once he has learned where 'heel' is you can use the command to return him to that position.

Recall

Once your dog knows his name, you need to train him to come back to you (recall) the instant you call him. This is essential for safety when he is off-leash and running free. If the dog knows that coming back to you means he will be rewarded, he is more likely to comply. Initially, the reward should be of high value, such as a really tasty treat or a prized toy. As your dog becomes conditioned to return to you on command, praise will probably be sufficient, but you can give occasional high-value rewards to maintain immediate response.

Top tips

- If your dog lags behind, it could be that you are walking too fast for him to keep up, so slow to his pace. Alternatively, it is because he is more interested in sniffing to see who has been along that way previously, and possibly in making his own passage. Don't let him 'train' you in this way, but insist he remains at heel.
- Always finish on a success. If the dog recalls the first time, end the lesson there, leaving him with a positive association. If you have difficulties teaching your dog to recall, consult a professional trainer for help. It is very important that your dog recalls when you want him to.

When your dog is obediently coming back to you the first time you call him, try the recall exercise in a group of one or two quiet dogs you both know. Approach the other (leashed) dogs with your dog on an extended, long leash. Before they meet and greet, call him back to you. If he responds, reward him lavishly; if not, simply reel him in, drop to one knee as he approaches, reward him as he reaches you and then try again. Once your dog is recalling well in this situation, try him off-leash, but use the leash if necessary. Eventually try the exercise with all the dogs off-leash.

1 *To begin recall training, walk forward with your dog on a long leash and at heel as usual. Then allow the leash to go slack and move backwards, calling your dog's name and the command 'come' at the same time. Offer a treat or high-value toy to elicit a quick response.*

2 *As the dog reaches you, say 'sit', and when he responds give the treat or play a game with a toy and praise him lavishly. Once he is responding instantly each time you do this exercise, try dropping the leash on the ground (within easy reach) to see what his reaction is. When you are happy that he will come to you immediately on command, try the exercise off-leash in a secure area, gradually increasing the distance between you.*

Sit

Four principles apply to training your dog in the sit position, and these may also be applied to heel-training:
- Attention
- Command
- Execute
- Reward

The acronym ACER will help you remember them.

Be patient when teaching the sit: dogs feel vulnerable in this position and, depending on your dog's history, he may not be very comfortable with it.

If you wish to use treat training to teach your dog to sit, then follow these instructions. Stand beside your dog with a treat in the hand closest to him. Offer the treat, then give the command 'sit' and at the same time move the treat up towards the dog's nose and over his head. Move the treat back slightly so the dog is looking up; he will automatically move into the sit position. As he does, reward him with the treat.

Top tip

When rewarding with a treat, do not hold it so high that the dog tries to jump up to get it. He will associate the reward with jumping up instead of the required sit position.

Top tip

To teach your dog to sit up and then stand from a lying position, put a treat under his nose and raise it above his head, simultaneously saying 'sit' or 'stand'. Reward him for the desired response. Practise each exercise separately at first and reward after each element. Then, request a sit, down, stay and follow with a reward. Finally, request all of these and a stand after the stay, then give a reward. This usually becomes a game that the dog really enjoys.

1 *Command 'sit' and simultaneously apply gentle pressure with your left hand on the dog's rear end to push him down.*

2 *Responding to the pressure, the dog will execute the command by sitting.*

3 *When he does so, reward him with the treat. Always request that your dog sits before feeding him or putting him on his leash. This will reinforce good manners, and also your 'number one' status.*

Stay

The ability to get your dog to stay where you want him, both indoors and out, is useful. For instance, you can use this command if you have visitors and you want your dog to remain in his bed out of the way, or if he needs to stay put for his own safety and that of others while on a walk.

The free stay

Once you are happy with your dog staying on the leash, you can progress to the free stay. To do this, move away from your dog, command 'stay' and drop the leash on the floor (put your foot on the leash if you are worried about him running off). Wait a few seconds, then walk to and around the dog, finishing by his right side. Reward him.

1 To teach stay, have the dog on a leash and put him into the sit position by your left heel.

2 To start, you are simply going to walk around the dog with him in a controlled stay, so command 'stay', with the leash slack in your left hand. Hold your right hand with the palm open in front of the dog (as shown) as a visual signal. Repeat the 'stay' command and then take one step to the side of the dog.

3 Repeat the command, then walk briskly around the dog, staying close to him so he knows where you are. Complete the circuit by standing at your dog's right side. Reward him with calm praise.

4 Repeat the exercise, this time moving a little further away at the front but coming close again at the back to reassure the dog you are still there. If he stays in position, you can gradually increase the distance between you.

Down and roll over

Once your dog has learned to sit (see page 118), the next step is to teach him to lie down on command, then roll onto his side. If your dog can do these things and will let you handle him all over, it is extremely handy for grooming, visits to the vet, or just when you want him to lie quietly while you are occupied with something else.

Using food treats wisely

A key element that forms the base for all training is food control; follow the procedure on page 115 as the method used to food-train puppies is exactly the same for adult dogs. However, dogs should not be rewarded with food treats for ever, or they will become fat. Use treats as part of the daily food ration, not in addition to it. Once your dog understands what you want, give food rewards only intermittently. At other times, give lavish verbal and physical praise, which your dog will appreciate just as much.

1 *With your dog in the sit position, get him to focus his attention on a treat in your hand.*

2 *Put the treat under his nose, then slowly move it down to the floor or between his front paws. He will sink to the floor in his effort to get the treat. As soon as he does, say 'down' and reward him with the treat and praise. Practise this a couple of times and you will find that your dog soon learns to lie down on command in anticipation of a reward.*

3 *If all goes well, try extending the lie down into a stay. As you step away from the lying dog, say 'stay' (with a hand signal as shown, if necessary), wait a couple of seconds, then go back to him and reward him lavishly. Gradually extend the distance between you and your dog as you command the stay. You will be surprised at how quickly he learns to do this.*

Roll over

With your dog in the down position, you can move on to the roll over exercise. Because exposing his tummy makes him feel vulnerable (to potential attackers), your dog will lie on his side or back only if he feels safe.

Top tip

Instant reward is essential when teaching down and roll over because a dog is at his most defenceless in a lying position. A reward will take his mind off that feeling and teach him that lying on command is pleasant and non-threatening. Be patient: if you get annoyed, the dog will sense it, and you are unlikely to achieve your goal. Some dogs take longer than others to feel at ease with these exercises.

1 *Show your dog a treat.*

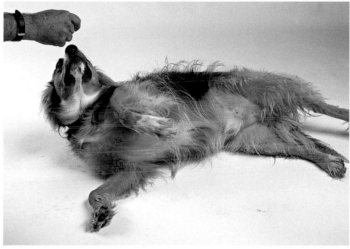

2 *Move the treat closer to his nose, then move it slowly around towards his shoulder, over the back of his neck and down.*

3 *The dog's head will follow your hand until he has to lie flat on his side to keep the treat in sight.*

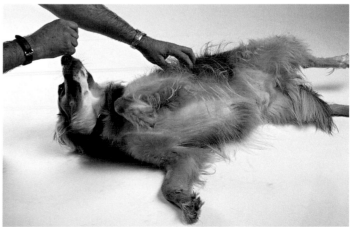

4 *At this point say 'roll over', and give your dog the treat and stroke his tummy. Practise until he learns that 'roll over' is a rewarding command to follow.*

1 Use an everyday (low-value) toy as the item to be retrieved, but have a high-value toy (one that your dog desires above all others) in your pocket, or hidden behind your back to use as the reward once your dog brings the other toy back to you. Have the dog at heel in a sit-stay position (see pages 118–119), then throw the low-value toy, saying 'fetch' at the same time.

2 Once the dog has the toy, call him back to you by saying his name and 'fetch'.

3 Praise the dog lavishly when he returns with the low-value toy, then play a game with the high-value toy. Your dog will soon get the message: no low-value toy, no game. Repeat once or twice, and finish on a win to keep your dog's retrieve motivation high.

Top tip

Don't expect the dog to understand the retrieve exercise immediately. He will probably be used to playing with his toys, not retrieving them and giving them to you.

Retrieve

Throwing a toy for your dog to retrieve is a good way to see that he gets adequate exercise, and it comprises a game that you will both enjoy. If a dog won't retrieve for you, how do you get him interested in playing 'fetch' in the first place?

If your dog won't let go of the toy, don't get into a tug-of-war situation. To make him release it, put him on the leash and command him to sit. Take hold of the toy, but do not pull it; place the thumb and forefinger of your free hand under the dog's muzzle. Apply gentle pressure to his jowls, pushing them up and over his bottom teeth. At the same time give the command 'give'. The dog will then release his grip and you will be able to take the toy. The intention, of course, is not to hurt the dog, but just to make him a bit uncomfortable until he releases the toy. After repeating this exercise a few times, you will find that as soon as you put your finger and thumb under his jaw, your dog will respond to the command 'give' and allow you to take the toy without a fuss. In future, you will simply be able to call the dog into the sit position, reach for the toy, say 'give' and he will release it into your hand.

Road safety

Knowing how to cross a road correctly with your dog is vital for everyone's safety. He should cross with you, not be dragged across by you, or you by him. There is obvious danger in an owner struggling across a road with a dog that is out of control. In order to be able to cross a road safely, your dog must obey the 'heel' and 'sit' commands (see pages 116 and 118). Only when your dog is sitting calmly and quietly by your side can you concentrate fully on the traffic to make sure the road is absolutely clear before you cross.

1 *If your dog is not used to traffic, accustom him to the sights and sounds by taking him to a spot where you can sit and watch traffic go by without being too close. Distract him by offering small pieces of food or a desirable toy. Do not fuss over him too much or cling on to him; that will just make him feel there is something to be afraid of. Speak to him calmly and in a normal tone.*

2 *Once your dog appears to be unbothered by traffic, walk him quietly along the pavement (it is safer to place yourself between your dog and traffic), again distracting him as vehicles approach. Reward him once they have passed. Soon he will look to you for a reward and take no notice of the moving traffic.*

3 *When crossing the road, stop at a point where you have a good view in both directions. Avoid crossing at corners and junctions, unless there is a pedestrian crossing. Command your dog to sit at the heel position while you check out whether the road is safe to cross. Continue to remind the dog to stay, keeping his attention on you with a treat, toy or verbal encouragement until you cross.*

4 *Cross only when the road is clear in both directions. Keep checking for approaching vehicles and keep your dog's attention on you by having a treat in the hand closest to him.*

Social skills

A dog who is well socialized with humans and other animals is less likely to develop behaviour problems. The principles of socializing puppies also apply to adult dogs.

If you have an adult dog who has not been socialized properly, you need to address this situation carefully and correctly. The best way to do this is to find a training school that holds socialization classes for older dogs in a safe and controlled environment. Doing this will make you feel more confident, too, especially if you have a dog who gets overexcited or even becomes aggressive when he meets people or other dogs, and you are not sure how to cope with the situation.

Having a dog who will sit and stay on command is the key to successful introduction, integration and interaction. If you can control your dog calmly, you stand a better chance of him accepting the situations around him so that interacting with other people and animals is more likely to be a positive experience for both of you.

A dog who is willing to play is a happy dog. Taking your dog to classes where he can socialize with others will bring out the best in him.

House manners

It is important that your dog understands his place in the household and behaves appropriately. For example, you should be able to greet visitors at the door without your dog rushing to get there first or refusing to let them in.

There are a number of things that you can do to implement house rules that your dog understands. When you come home at any time of day, do what you need to do first, such as taking off your coat and hanging it up or putting the groceries away. Do anything at all except go straight to your dog and give him attention. While he is rushing around in excitement at your return and demanding attention, ignore him. You don't want to reinforce his notion that he has high status in the household. After a while your dog will get fed up with being ignored and will either find something to do or lie down. At this point, call him and give him a few minutes of attention.

Make sure that the rest of the family, and guests, also adopt this strategy. When family members or

Did you know ...?

Human beings believe that, because they look and feel guilty about doing something wrong, so does a dog. This is not true. A prime example is the dog who has soiled in the house. Since defecation and urination are natural functions for a dog, why should he feel guilt? The dog's timid appearance when you come home to a dirty floor is not due to his guilt, but to your angry tone of voice and hostile body language. Instead of being annoyed at the dog, you should be cross with yourself for having put the dog in the position where he had no choice but to relieve himself inside. Aim to solve such a 'problem' by asking yourself how it could have been prevented. How old is the dog? Could he reasonably be expected to last the length of time you were gone without needing to relieve himself? More importantly, ask yourself if you have toilet-trained your dog correctly so he knows where to go.

Top tip

Remember to be consistent with house rules so that the dog does not become confused; not allowing him to do something one day and then allowing it the next may result in the formation of stress- or anxiety-induced behaviour.

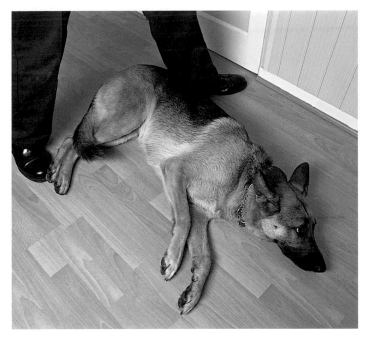

A typical example of a dog with no house manners: you need to go from one room to another but, as you get up, the dog also gets up and stands or lies in the doorway, blocking your exit. You end up either trying to move him out of the way or stepping over him. This is a mistake, as you are deferring to the dog and thereby elevating his status.

Try to pre-empt the behaviour and deal with it before it becomes a problem. As you are getting up from your seat, give the dog a 'stay' command, which tells him what you want him to do. Provided you have taught him what this command means, he will obey. If the dog is already standing or lying in the doorway, tell him to move away using the 'away' command; do not step over him.

guests sit down, they should be asked to ignore the dog. If he tries to get on someone's lap or a chair, gently but firmly push him down without saying anything to him. Even a reprimand would fulfil his desire for attention. After a few minutes, he will go away. Leave him for a further few minutes and then call him to you, using his name and the command 'come'. Give him a bit of attention, then gently push him away with the command 'finish', and remove your hands and arms from his reach.

By introducing these few firm rules, you will soon see a change in your dog's behaviour. He will not always be demanding your attention or be under your feet. When in the house you have the right to sit and read, relax or work; it is simply bad manners for your dog to put himself in your way or refuse to move.

Solving behavioural problems

'Why does my dog misbehave?' is the most common question dog trainers are asked. Think about it – is your dog really misbehaving, or is he doing what he thinks is the right thing? The main reason why dogs 'misbehave' is because they have been forced into behaving in that way because humans have failed to train and stimulate them sufficiently. It is important, however, before embarking on a retraining programme, that you get your dog checked out by a vet to establish that there is no physical reason for the problem behaviour.

There is often no quick-fix solution where some behavioural difficulties are concerned, such as aggression, chasing other animals and problems with car travel, so you have to be prepared for a prolonged and sustained programme of retraining, as well as enlisting the professional help of a dog trainer.

Top tip

All areas of obedience-training require continual reinforcement to ensure that both you and your dog stay sharp.

Climbing on furniture

If you don't want your dog to sit on furniture, set a precedent and don't let him do it in the first place (from puppyhood), otherwise he will think it is his right to get on furniture whenever he likes.

1 *If your dog won't get off furniture when commanded to, hook your finger into his collar to take control and say 'off'.*

2 *If the dog still won't move, gently but firmly remove him, repeating the command 'off'. If he tries to jump back on, sharply command 'no'. If he tries again, again say 'no' and put him out of the room. Let him back in a short time later and tell him to lie down; if he tries to get back on the furniture, put him out of the room again. He will learn that getting on furniture is unrewarding (he is put out of the room and away from you), whereas by not doing so he is allowed to remain in the room with you.*

Attention seeking

If your dog demands your attention by jumping up and pawing at your legs while you are doing something else, such as trying to read, you should ignore him.

2 *The dog will then lie down quietly while deciding what his next move should be.*

1 When he gets no reaction from you, he will sit down and consider the situation.

3 Soon after he lies down, it is important that you reward this desired behaviour. This way, the dog will associate non-attention-seeking behaviour with a pleasant, positive experience, and learn that leaping around trying to get attention brings no reward.

Chewing

Dogs who chew things they shouldn't can soon wreck a house and its contents, so it's essential to put a stop to this destructive behaviour swiftly.

Have a number of rattle pots (lidded containers half-filled with pebbles or large dry beans) accessible around the house to use when you see your dog chewing inappropriately.

If your dog enjoys chewing particular items, such as shoes, table legs or soft furnishings, buy a non-toxic anti-chew spray (available from pet stores) and treat those items with it. Then encourage your dog to have a nibble. He will find this most unrewarding because of the very unpleasant taste and won't be likely to try it again.

2 Quickly replace the item that your dog is chewing with a toy or a chew treat that he can nibble on instead. Encourage him to take it and chew it.

1 Throw a rattle pot so it lands near your pet (obviously don't aim to hit him with it) to interrupt the chewing. As it lands, the dog will stop chewing or jump away in surprise. If you don't feel confident about your aim, or have a very nervous dog, simply shake the pot hard instead to make a loud noise.

3 Give the dog an activity toy filled with something tasty to keep him occupied, especially if you are busy, so he doesn't get bored and go looking for something inappropriate to chew for entertainment.

HEALTH CARE

The dog, like all mammals, has a skeleton that shelters his internal organs, enabling him to process food and reproduce. Powerful muscles are attached to the skeleton to enable motion. The dog mates with the opposite sex and the female bears live young which are suckled and reared by the mother until they are able to survive alone. All dogs, whatever their breed, share the physiology (way in which a living creature functions); they differ only in minor ways to produce a larger, smaller, more compact or elongated conformation, with some displaying anomalies of fur, balance, physical advantages or limitations, or bone structure caused by particular mutations or selective breeding.

Most behavioural and medical problems are caused by the attitude of owners towards their dogs. You can avoid them by making sure that you do all you can to understand and work positively with canine behaviour, as well as by providing your dog with a good diet and adequate exercise, and by being aware of early symptoms that all is not well with your pet.

In addition, some ailments are caused by inappropriate breed requirements for showing purposes, or by careless breeding programmes, whereby unnatural physical attributes are created and perpetuated because it is the 'fashion' or because care has not been taken to ensure that parents are of sound and healthy breeding stock. The canine body is a remarkable feat of natural engineering that has evolved, in the main, into an animal possessing great beauty, grace, intelligence and athletic prowess. To keep your pet in the peak of condition it helps to know:
• how your pet's body is constructed
• how it works
• how to recognize when something is wrong
• what to do when your dog is ill or injured

From routine parasite control to vaccination, reproduction to neutering, this section tells you all you need to know about canine physiology and health throughout your dog's life.

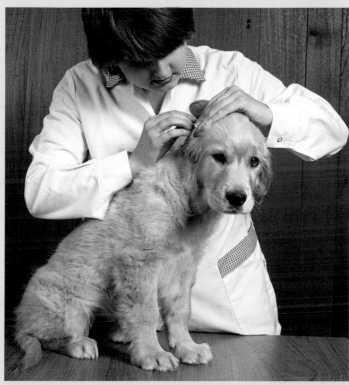
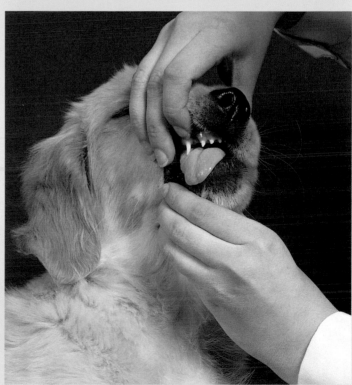

The canine body

Whatever the breed, dogs are carnivorous, athletic and, in general, characterized by the qualities on the checklist. They have four toes and nails on their front and back paws, plus a fifth toe (known as the dewclaw) that serves no useful purpose; dewclaws are absent on the front limbs of certain breeds. Dogs have 42 teeth – 20 in the upper jaw and 22 in the lower.

Checklist

✓ great powers of endurance
✓ exceptional hearing
✓ a superior sense of smell
✓ dense fur
✓ whiskers
✓ athleticism

The skeleton

The skeleton comprises a semi-rigid framework that supports other softer structures. A system of efficient levers to aid movement comprises the bones of the spine, limbs, shoulders and pelvis (working together with muscles and tendons), while the skull, ribcage and pelvis protect the major organs they contain. Bones are joined together to form the skeleton via tendons and ligaments. Four distinct types of bone make up the skeleton – long, short, irregular and flat bones. Each has a particular function.

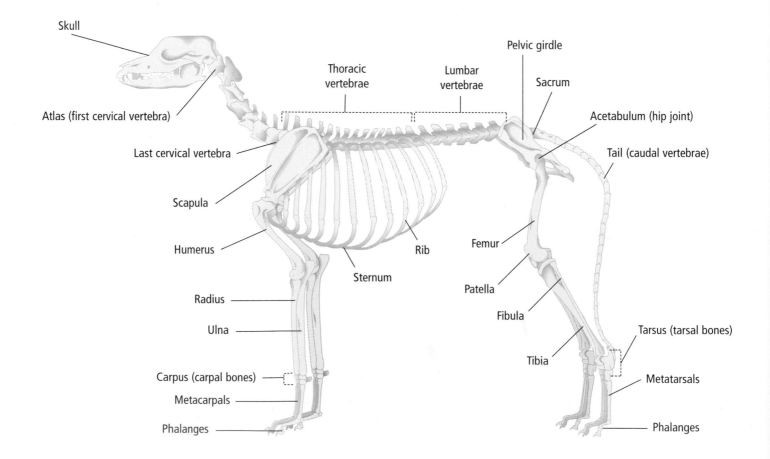

Skull
Atlas (first cervical vertebra)
Last cervical vertebra
Scapula
Humerus
Radius
Ulna
Carpus (carpal bones)
Metacarpals
Phalanges
Thoracic vertebrae
Lumbar vertebrae
Sternum
Rib
Pelvic girdle
Sacrum
Acetabulum (hip joint)
Tail (caudal vertebrae)
Femur
Patella
Fibula
Tibia
Tarsus (tarsal bones)
Metatarsals
Phalanges

Long bones

These long bones are cylindrical and have hollow shafts that contain the vital bone marrow in which the manufacture of all blood cells takes place. They form the dog's limbs, comprising the humerus, radius, femur, tibia and fibula.

Short bones

These short bones consist of a spongy core surrounded by compact bone. They comprise the feet bones and patella (kneecap – where the femur joins the tibia).

Irregular bones

So called because of their irregular shapes, these bones are similar in structure to short bones. A long string of irregular bones make up the spine (vertebral column) and tail. The irregular projections of the spinal column serve as attachment points for the various muscles of the back.

Flat bones

These are made of two layers of compact bone with a spongy layer sandwiched between them, and comprise the skull, pelvis and shoulder blades (scapulae). Flattened and elongated bones make up the dog's 13 pairs of ribs; these bones contain a substantial amount of marrow that produces a proportion of blood cells.

The muscular system

Overlying the skeletal framework is a complex network of muscles that gives the dog its powerful and athletic movement and capacity for endurance as opposed to speed. There are three types of muscle in the canine body:

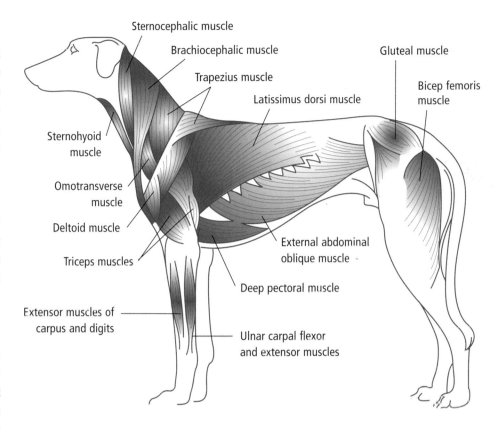

Sternocephalic muscle
Brachiocephalic muscle
Trapezius muscle
Gluteal muscle
Latissimus dorsi muscle
Bicep femoris muscle
Sternohyoid muscle
Omotransverse muscle
Deltoid muscle
Triceps muscles
External abdominal oblique muscle
Deep pectoral muscle
Extensor muscles of carpus and digits
Ulnar carpal flexor and extensor muscles

• **Striped (striated) muscles** (see above) comprise muscle tissue in which the contractile fibres are arranged in parallel bundles, and are attached to the limbs and other parts of the anatomy which are under the voluntary control of the dog, such as movement. These are known as voluntary muscles. Voluntary muscles are usually attached to bones that form a joint. Extensor muscles extend and straighten a limb, while flexor muscles flex and bend the joint. Muscles that move a limb away from the body are called abductors, and adductor muscles move them back in again.

• **Smooth (unstriated) muscles** carry out muscular functions not under the dog's voluntary control, such as the muscles of the intestines and walls of blood vessels. These are called involuntary muscles.

• **The specialized cardiac muscle** has adapted to carry out the functions of the heart. It possesses unique powers of rhythmic contraction to pump blood around the body via a network of blood vessels.

Ligaments and tendons

Ligaments are short bands of tough, fibrous connective tissue that connect bones or cartilages, or hold together a joint; they also comprise membranous folds that support organs and keep them in position.

Tendons are flexible but inelastic cords of strong, fibrous tissue attaching muscles to bone.

The respiratory system

Respiration provides the dog's body with the oxygen that is vital for life, and expels waste products (in the form of carbon dioxide gas) from the blood. During respiration, the dog draws in air through his nasal passages via the nose and mouth. This air passes through the throat (pharynx) and down the windpipe (trachea), through the bronchi and into the lungs. Gaseous exchange takes place in the lungs, whereby carbon dioxide from the blood filters into the air sacs, to be exhaled, as oxygen passes from inhaled air to replenish the blood. Used air is then exhaled. Breathing is automatic: chest muscles contract and relax, acting like a pump on the ribs and diaphragm, driving air in and out of the lungs.

Did you know ...?

Panting is another function connected with the respiratory system. It serves a useful purpose in drawing cold air in over the tongue and passing it out again, thus reducing body heat by water evaporation from the tongue.

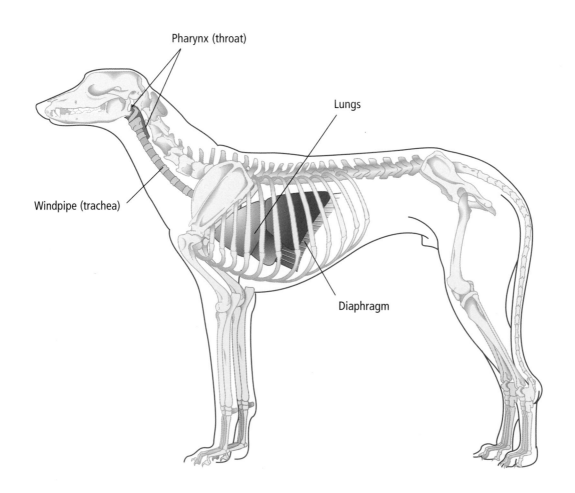

Pharynx (throat)

Lungs

Windpipe (trachea)

Diaphragm

The circulatory system

Every body cell needs a supply of nourishment, and this is delivered via the blood, which also removes waste products from the body. Blood comprises red blood cells and white blood corpuscles that are contained in a fluid called plasma. Plasma contains platelets which contain a blood-clotting agent in the event of cuts and wounds. Red blood cells transport oxygen and nutrients derived from food, while white blood corpuscles collect and transport impurities and bacteria that have invaded the red cells.

Incredible journey

Blood is continually pumped around the body via the four-chambered heart, its journey beginning in the left auricle (upper chamber). Oxygen-enriched blood travels from the left auricle into the left ventricle (lower chamber) and on into a great artery (aorta) to run quickly through all the arteries distributing its store of oxygen and nutrients collected from the small intestine. As it releases its 'goodies', the blood also collects waste matter comprising bacteria, dead blood cells and carbon dioxide. The blood then enters veins where,

Top tip

Blood passing through the aorta causes its walls to expand and a pressure wave pass down the arteries – this is known as the 'pulse'.

laden with waste products, it begins to slow down on its way back to the lungs to dump its rubbish and be replenished with oxygen and nutrients, before passing on into the heart to repeat its journey.

Red = oxygenated blood (left side of the heart)

Blue = deoxygenated blood (right side of the heart)

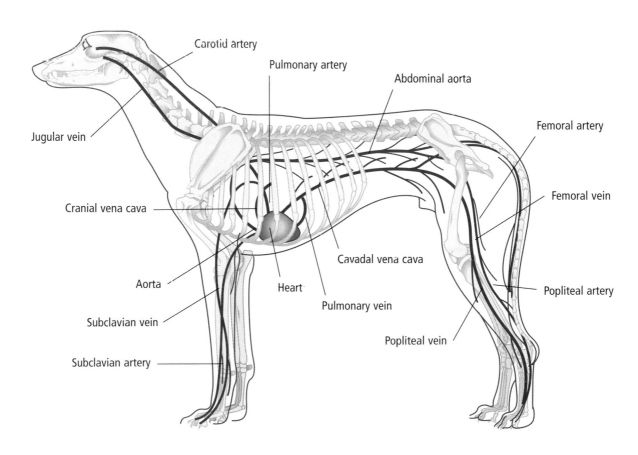

Carotid artery

Pulmonary artery

Abdominal aorta

Femoral artery

Jugular vein

Cranial vena cava

Femoral vein

Aorta

Cavadal vena cava

Heart

Pulmonary vein

Popliteal artery

Subclavian vein

Popliteal vein

Subclavian artery

The digestive system

Simply put, the alimentary canal is a type of tube of varying size that runs through the dog from the mouth at one end, to the anal opening at the other. Food enters via the mouth and passes through the tube, where it is digested and all the available nutrients are extracted; what remains is then excreted.

The tongue laps up fluids and licks up food particles, while the teeth bite at and pick up food to chew it. Swallowing food is aided by saliva, which is produced from three pairs of salivary glands that empty into the mouth. From the mouth food and liquids pass down the oesophagus (gullet) into the stomach. There, acids and enzymes break down the food into chyme (mixture of partly digested food and gastric juices), which then passes through into the small intestine where useful nutrients are absorbed into the bloodstream. The liver aids in the digestive process and neutralizes toxins.

Once everything of value (fats, sugars, minerals, vitamins, proteins and carbohydrates) has been extracted in the small intestine, the remaining matter passes into the large intestine where excess fluid is removed via the kidneys and bladder to be voided as urine (through the penis in males and the vulva in bitches), before it moves on into the rectum and out of the body through the anus as faeces.

Did you know ...?

A dog's stomach contains powerful enzymes that allow them to eat rotten meat and other foods without becoming ill.

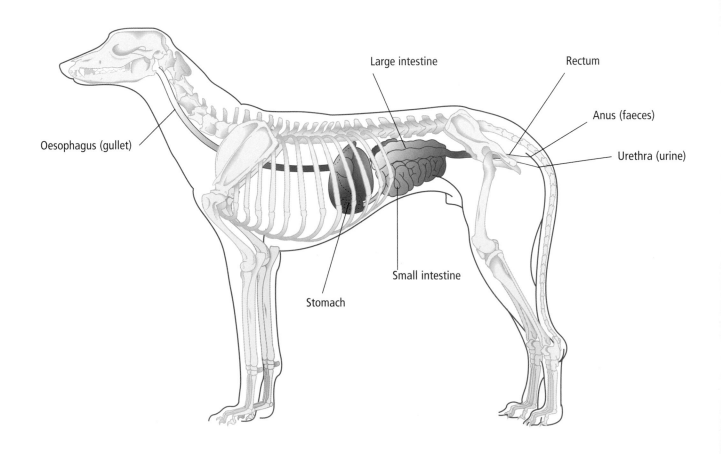

Oesophagus (gullet)

Large intestine

Rectum

Anus (faeces)

Urethra (urine)

Stomach

Small intestine

Skin and fur

A thin layer of tissue – the skin – forms the natural outer covering of the dog's body, and serves a number of functions:

• it keeps out foreign bodies
• it keeps in moisture
• it regulates body temperature
• it manufactures vitamin D
• it protects against ultraviolet radiation via skin pigment and hair
• it contains glands (which play an important role in expelling waste products from the body), and receptors for pain, temperature and pressure.

The skin is composed of three layers, the epidermis being the outermost layer, the dermis below that, and the hypodermis being the innermost layer, below which is a layer of fat which serves as insulation, a back-up nutrient supply, and protection for the bones and organs underneath. Unlike us, dogs do not sweat through glands in the skin, except for a few in the feet.

Canine hair is formed from epidermis. It grows through a tube called the hair follicle. For each hair follicle, there is a sebaceous gland

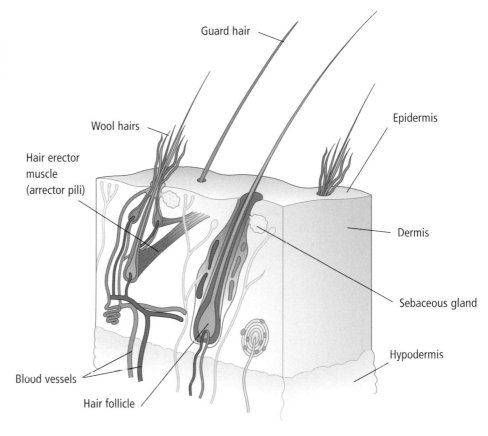

Guard hair

Wool hairs

Hair erector muscle (arrector pili)

Epidermis

Dermis

Sebaceous gland

Hypodermis

Blood vessels

Hair follicle

which secretes an oily, semi-liquid substance (sebum) to lubricate and waterproof the hair and skin. These glands also produce a scent that the dog uses as a marker for his territory, as well as secrete chemical signals called pheromones that help attract members of the opposite sex.

There are three types of hair:
• **guard hairs** (top coat) are the long waterproofed hairs of the top layer of the coat
• **wool hairs** (undercoat) trap air in the coat to help keep the dog warm
• **vibrissae** (whiskers) are hairs that are sensitive to touch, found around the mouth, eyes and on each cheek

Moulting occurs when the dog sheds hair in order to have a coat suitable for the ambient temperature, so he does not overheat. The coat will grow and thicken in cold temperatures to help him stay warm enough. The epidermis is constantly being replaced as tissue cells die, and sloughs away into tiny flakes of dandruff (dead skin).

Changes in skin colour

In a fit, healthy dog, the skin is pliable; in a sick or dehydrated dog, it is stiff and unyielding. A sudden change from the normal pale pink colouring can indicate illness and needs veterinary investigation. Any change of colour in the dog's skin is usually first noticed on the lips and gums.
• **White** can indicate anaemia due to parasite infestation, dietary deficiency or even shock
• **Reddening** indicates inflammatory disease of the skin or underlying tissues
• **Blue** indicates heart trouble, respiratory disease or poisoning
• **Yellow** indicates jaundice (liver dysfunction)

Canine senses

A dog's nervous and sensory systems are essential to his health and well-being. Perceptions and reactions to his environment are dependent on his senses; movement is controlled through the central nervous system (the brain and spinal cord); and the endocrine system (the hormone-producing glands) controls his patterns of behaviour. The checklist shows the five bodily senses through which a dog perceives his surroundings.

Checklist
- ✓ sight
- ✓ smell
- ✓ hearing
- ✓ taste
- ✓ touch

Sight

Canine vision is inferior to humans during the day, but is superior at night. Dogs do see colours, but not as distinctly as humans (in pastel as opposed to strong colours), and their peripheral vision is better than ours.

In addition to the upper and lower eyelids, there is a third eyelid – the nictitating membrane (haw), which is comprised of a thin sheet of pale tissue tucked away in the corner of the eye. Its function is to help remove dust and dirt from the surface of the

eye (cornea) by moving across it during any inward movement, and also to help keep the eyeball moist and lubricated. The eyes are also used to communicate – staring eyes indicate a threat, while 'sad eyes' or looking away indicate submission.

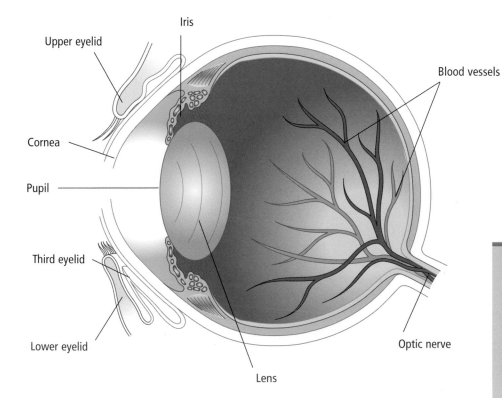

Iris

Upper eyelid

Cornea

Pupil

Third eyelid

Lower eyelid

Lens

Blood vessels

Optic nerve

Did you know ...?

A dog's vision is not as detailed as ours, and he recognizes different objects by smell and shape rather than by texture and detail.

Smell

A dog's primary sense is his sense of smell, as it is essential in relation to his sex life and hunting for food and water. The area in a dog's nose for detecting scent is nearly 37 times larger than that in humans, and therefore is approximately 100 times more powerful than a human's. The parts of the brain that process signals coming in from the nose are far greater in size and complexity in a dog than are the corresponding parts of the human brain.

A special organ in the roof of the mouth – the vomeronasal (or Jacobson's) organ – 'tastes' certain smells (such as that exuded by a bitch in season) to help the dog analyse and react to them faster. When the dog is using this organ, he will draw in mouthfuls of air and appear to be 'tasting' it.

When two dogs meet they will usually smell each other's face and then their inguinal regions. Scent plays a significant part in territory. When a male dog marks a prominent object with urine, he is deliberately masking the smell of dogs that have recently passed by, and thereby stamping his claim as 'top dog' in that territory. Faeces are also used as scent markers, with the anal glands discharging a foul-smelling substance unique to that dog.

A dog will use his keen sense of smell to satisfy his curiosity about something.

Canine fact

Dogs predominantly use their noses and mouths to find out about their world, whereas humans use their eyes and hands. Keeping eye and hand contact to a minimum when greeting dogs can reduce their fear and help us to make friends with them more quickly.

Hearing

A dog's hearing is vastly superior to that of a human and he is, therefore, more sensitive to sounds than we are – especially those at high frequencies which we cannot hear (hence the use of 'silent' dog whistles). A dog's mobile ears help to pinpoint the source of a sound, since they can be directed towards it. As well as hearing sounds, a dog's ears are also used to communicate via their position to indicate aggression (back), interest (pricked) and submission (down).

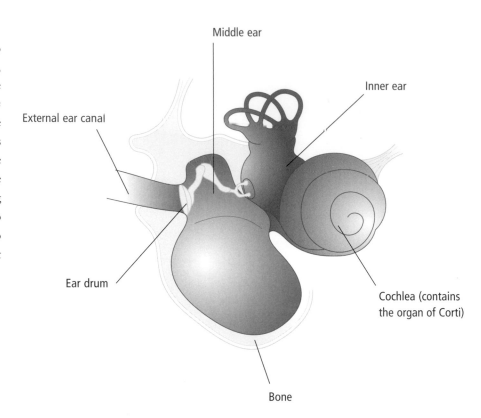

Middle ear

Inner ear

External ear canal

Ear drum

Cochlea (contains the organ of Corti)

Bone

Dogs with pricked ears can orientate them more easily to pinpoint the source of a sound accurately, whereas this is more difficult for dogs with big, hanging ear flaps which can only be slightly raised.

Taste

Whereas humans have taste buds, situated on the tongue, that differentiate between sweet, sour, salty and bitter tastes, the canine sense of taste is thought not to be as well developed – only about one-sixth as sensitive as that of humans.

Most dogs thoroughly enjoy using their keen sense of smell to track and find toys thrown for them.

Frequently asked question

 Q How many teeth does a dog have?

A A total of 42, made up of:
- 8 premolars in the lower jaw (4 per side) and 6 in the upper (3 per side)
- 6 molars (3 per side) in the upper jaw and 6 (3 per side) in the lower
- 6 incisors in the lower jaw and 6 in the upper jaw
- 2 canine teeth on the lower jaw and 2 on the upper

Occasionally, double dentition is seen when milk teeth are not shed. This may necessitate veterinary intervention to remove the problem milk teeth so that they do not interfere with secondary (permanent) tooth growth and action, which could ultimately reflect upon efficient digestion and lead to health problems.

Touch

Dogs use their noses, mouths and paws to examine objects, after first checking them out by smell. The skin is the main touch receptor, and different breeds and types of dogs are more touch-sensitive than others. Dogs that have not been well handled since puppyhood tend to shy away from being touched in sensitive areas, such as the feet, mouth, head, between the hind legs and tails (these areas being vulnerable if attacked).

Routine health care

Keeping an eye on your dog's demeanour, and carrying out simple health checks on a regular basis, will enable you to monitor his state of health. Things to look out for are shown on the checklist.

Checklist

✓ general condition, skin and coat
✓ appetite and thirst
✓ mouth and teeth
✓ ears, eyes and nose
✓ weight
✓ faeces and urine (eliminations)
✓ ease of movement

Teaching your dog to have his head and mouth handled pays dividends when it comes to checking his teeth and gums regularly.

• See pages 28–29 for at-a-glance signs of a healthy and unhealthy dog.
• See pages 90–93 for advice on body condition, vital signs eliminations, general demeanour and at-a-glance maintenance checks.
• See page 135 for top tips on skin condition.

Daily checks

Some dogs are more stoical than others and will put up with considerable discomfort and pain before their owners realize something is wrong. This is why it is so essential to check your dog over thoroughly every day for any unusual lumps and sore spots. Check his eyes and mouth for foreign bodies or any sign of inflammation, and watch for irregularities in behaviour, eating and excretion.

Mouth and teeth

Dog breath should not be offensive – tooth decay is easy to diagnose because of the resulting unpleasant smell. The mouth area and tongue should be salmon pink in colour – white gums indicate anaemia, red bleeding gums are an indication of gingivitis (see page 165) and blue/grey gums suggest a circulatory problem. If your dog shows a reluctance to eat or drink, seek veterinary advice.

Nose, ears and eyes

The nose should be clean, slightly damp and free from discharge. The inner ear surface should be clean, smooth and odour-free. Smelly or dirty ears need veterinary investigation, as this suggests that infection is present.

The eyes should be clear, bright and free from discharge. Some brachycephalic (broad-headed) breeds often suffer from eye discharge; this is a result of the skull structure being deformed, meaning that tears cannot drain away as they would normally. Tearstains can be removed with cotton wool dipped in clean, boiled and cooled water, and you can also buy proprietary tearstain removers. Any clouding of the eye surface requires veterinary attention, since this is usually the result of injury or cataract formation. The pupils should be of the same size, and the third eyelid retracted.

Ease of movement

Stiffness usually indicates joint problems, and limping suggests a direct pain source such as a fractured limb, a wound, a thorn stuck in the foot pad, or an infected nail bed. A reluctance to move combined with crying out when you attempt to move the dog may be due to an internal injury or ailment.

Veterinary health checks

Choose a vet who specializes in canine health and cultivate a good relationship with them. An owner who takes their pet for regular health checks and routine vaccinations, and seeks advice on parasite control and dental care, is a valued customer for whom a vet will be prepared to have more time. Keeping a diary of your dog's behaviour and health and, therefore, being able to explain any changes you have noticed in detail, is very useful in helping your vet treat your pet appropriately and swiftly when the need arises.

Veterinary surgeries and animal hospitals have reception areas where you can make appointments, pay bills and ask for advice. Many also sell canine equipment and run puppy socialization and regular weight-watching clinics.

If for any reason you feel you would like a second veterinary opinion, then it is within your right to ask for one; no one vet knows all there is to know about their particular field of work. Your vet may even suggest that they consult another expert in order to treat your dog appropriately.

Take your dog for a check-up at least once a year (combine this with the annual vaccination booster), and every six months for elderly pets, as this can often identify health problems before they become serious.

Frequently asked question

Q How often should I clean my dog's ears, and how do I do it?

A If the insides of the ears are looking dirty due to an accumulation of wax, but are not exuding an offensive odour (which requires veterinary treatment), simply gently wipe them out with cotton wool moistened with a few drops of olive or liquid paraffin oil.

If your dog scratches himself constantly, check his coat for signs of fleas.

Controlling fleas and ticks

There are various product options for flea and tick control and prevention available from vets, comprising sprays which are effective for up to three months), spot-ons (effective for one month, also called drop-ons) and pills (effective for one month). One particular flea product will also kill roundworm.

Fleas bite the dog's skin in order to feed off their blood, with the resulting bites causing intense itching that can lead to severe dermatitis. Heavy flea infestation can cause anaemia, leading to death if left untreated.

Ticks are blood-sucking parasites that cause itchiness, infection and even paralysis in some countries. Never try to pull a tick off the skin or its head may be left embedded, which will lead to infection. A dab of surgical spirit or flea spray that also kills ticks will make them release their grip.

Parasite control

Dogs can suffer from a variety of external and internal parasites, including fleas, mites, lice, fungal infections, ticks and worms – all of which cause ill health. A wide variety of preparations designed to treat these parasites are available to buy from supermarkets and pet stores, but they are not as effective (nor often as easy to apply or administer) as those which are available on prescription from your vet. You must also treat other pets in the house, and the house itself, with treatments (also available from vets), or reinfestation will occur immediately. Vacuum-clean carpets and the place where your dog sleeps regularly, and wash your pet's bedding weekly or so to destroy flea eggs.

Intestinal worms (roundworm and tapeworm) are most efficiently controlled by an all-in-one treatment prescribed by your vet. See the 'Frequently asked question' on page 97 for when it is advisable to treat your dog for worms. Deworming products available from vets come in granule, pill, liquid or paste form.

Administering internal medication

Only give medication as prescribed or advised by your vet, and administer any medicines or pills strictly as directed.

If you are given a course of treatment for your dog, then ensure you complete it. If the treatment course is incomplete, then it is not likely to have the desired effect. This is not only a waste of your money, but your dog will continue to suffer unnecessarily. If you have difficulty getting your dog to take his medicine, then ask your vet for advice and/or help.

Liquids

Using a syringe (your vet can supply this) is often the easiest way to give liquid medicine to your dog. Simply insert the nozzle in the corner of the mouth and squeeze out the contents a little at a time, stroking your dog's throat to encourage him to swallow.

Pills

Some dogs will eat pills straight from your hand, or embedded in a morsel of tasty food. If these cannot be given in food, then follow these steps:
• hold your dog firmly
• tip back his head
• open his mouth
• pop the pill at the back of his throat
• close his mouth
• stroke his throat to encourage him to swallow the pill

Applying topical (external) treatments

Only use treatments prescribed or advised by your vet, and apply them strictly as directed. When administering drops or ointment to the eyes, hold the dog's head still (or get someone to hold him for you) and aim for the centre of the eye, or wherever directed by your vet.

To apply ear drops, hold the head still, squeeze in the drops as directed, then gently massage the base of the ear to ensure the liquid is evenly distributed on the affected area. When applying ointment to wounds, gently massage it into the affected area with a clean finger. In cases of zoonotic diseases (see page 171), wear rubber or plastic gloves for each topical application and dispose of them safely in the rubbish bin afterwards.

Vaccinations

Dogs, like every other mammal, are susceptible to certain viral diseases, some of which can prove fatal. While they will not pass these on to humans (apart from rabies), they will transfer them to other dogs, and also cats in the case of the *Bordetella bronchiseptica* (Bb) bacterium (responsible for kennel cough – see page 167). It is advisable to have your

dog vaccinated for the following reasons:
• to help prevent him dying prematurely
• to help prevent spread of disease
• to help eliminate canine viral diseases
• to enable you to book your dog into a boarding kennels when you go on vacation
• to enable you to travel abroad with your dog if required
• to enable you to enter your dog into dog shows and agility competitions

When to vaccinate

Vaccinations are given by injection (except the kennel cough vaccine which is squirted up the nose to protect against Bb bacteria and the para-influenza virus; the latter is also contained in the annual booster injection). Puppies and dogs that have not been vaccinated before need an initial course of vaccinations, comprising two injections 2–4 weeks apart. The second jab cannot be given before 10 weeks of age, but the first can be given as early as 6 weeks. Multiple vaccines are usually given in one injection which protects the dog against:
• canine distemper (D)
• canine adenovirus (CAV-2; hepatitis; H)
• parvovirus (P)
• para-influenza (Pi)
• leptospirosis (*L. canicola* and *L. icterohaemorrhagiae*; L)

Immunity for distemper and hepatitis lasts longer than immunity for the other diseases, so an alternating booster jab programme is usually employed whereby immunity to the DHPPi components are given one year and only the PPi and L components the following year. The rabies jab is given separately – routinely in some countries, but not in others that are rabies-free. However, a rabies vaccination is required when taking your dog abroad.

Did you know ...?

Some medicines can be added to or crushed up in food, while others can't, as doing this will affect their efficacy – ask your vet's advice regarding this.

Neutering

You may decide that you want to breed from your dog, and in this case you will know whether you want to raise puppies or set up a stud. If your dog is to be a pet only, however, then he or she should be neutered – whether male or female – in order to help prevent the problems in the checklist.

Checklist

- ✓ unwanted puppies
- ✓ potential behavioural problems
- ✓ cancer and other reproductive ailments
- ✓ the spread of disease
- ✓ straying
- ✓ females coming into season
- ✓ health risks during pregnancy and birth

Puppies are undeniably cute, but unless you are an experienced and responsible breeder, or are at least prepared to consider all the pros and cons beforehand, leave breeding to the experts.

Why neutering is a good idea

The urge to reproduce and pass on their genes to the next generation is intense in unneutered dogs. Both bitches and dogs will be strongly motivated to get to each other at the

appropriate time. When sexually mature, an unneutered dog will tend to wander, if he gets the chance, in search of potential mates, risking getting involved in traffic accidents or being picked up as a stray by a dog warden.

An unneutered bitch will come into season twice a year (although some breeds, such as the Basenji, only do so once a year) and must then be kept under tight control to avoid unwanted pregnancies, since she will always be on the lookout during these times to get out and mate.

If they can't get out, unneutered dogs will often go off their food, soil in the house, be extremely restless and whine in frustration.

When to neuter

Neutering (spaying in females and castration in males) should be done when the dog reaches sexual maturity at around 6 months old (the equivalent of an adolescent human), and at any time afterwards. Individual vets have their own policy on when to spay bitches: some prefer to let them have one season beforehand and spay at around 9 months of age in order to limit incidences of urinary incontinence afterwards; and some do not spay if a bitch is in season, preferring to wait until 3 months or so afterwards. This is due to the reproductive organs being enlarged with an increased supply of blood during the season and for a while afterwards, so there can be greater risks involved in the surgery.

Male dogs are difficult to keep confined if they scent a bitch in season and will risk life and limb trying to get to her. Sometimes the lengths they will go to in order to escape are amazing.

Canine fact

Male dogs can smell the pheromones produced by a bitch in season from a distance of up to 5km (3 miles) – so it is no wonder a bitch may attract a large gathering of likely suitors at this time. Visiting males will loiter around her territory and you will have to put up with their persistence in trying to get to her, and in hers in trying to get out to them. There may be fights in the vicinity between rival males, as well as barking and howling day and night.

Did you know ...?

Entire male dogs are often more independent than females, so can sometimes be more difficult to control, and bitches are generally considered to be more affectionate – although there are always exceptions to the rule.

What's involved

Because the operation is more involved in female dogs, the neutering procedure is more expensive than for males.

Females

The ovaries, Fallopian tubes and uterus are removed under a general anaesthetic. The operation site is shaved and cleaned to help prevent infection, and then a small incision is made mid-line (from the navel towards the hind legs) in order to remove the relevant organs. The wound is closed by means of stitches that are removed about 10–14 days later, unless soluble suture material is used, which gradually dissolves on its own.

Males

The dog is anaesthetized and his testicles (testes) and a small section of the spermatic cords are removed through a small incision in the scrotum; the incision is then stitched as for females.

Pre- and post-op care

The dog must go without food and water for 12 hours before the operation. Most males are back to normal in about 3 days, bitches in 5, and completely themselves again by the time they have their stitches out. When you bring your pet home from the vet's, he will probably still be drowsy from the anaesthetic, so put him in a warm, quiet place to rest undisturbed – with water and a light meal of cooked white fish or chicken – until he feels ready to join in the family activities again. Gently discourage the dog from nibbling or excessively licking the stitches (you may need to put an elizabethan collar on him if he persists in worrying the wound). If you have any worries at all following neutering, contact your vet for advice.

Neuter behaviour

If neutered as early as possible, the behaviour of male and female dogs will be almost the same – at least from the practical point of view of an owner, as both sexes tend to be more affectionate and amenable. There is some truth in the observation that neuters become more inactive than entires as they age (although their life expectancy is greater) due to them putting on weight. To prevent this happening, you may have to adjust your pet's diet and ensure he gets sufficient exercise. Sometimes bitches can become incontinent after they have been spayed, but this can usually be treated successfully with medication; on the plus side though, spaying does reduce a bitch's chance of developing mammary tumours.

Spaying and castration

Spaying

Before spaying: the female reproductive tract comprises the ovaries, Fallopian tubes and uterus (womb).

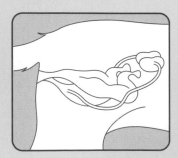

After spaying: the ovaries, Fallopian tubes and uterus are removed.

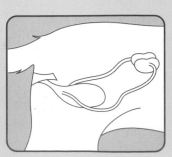

Castration

Before castration: the male reproductive tract comprises 2 testicles in a skin sac (scrotum), connected to the penis via the vas deferens (spermatic cords).

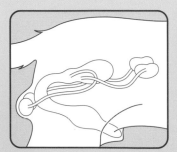

After castration: the testicles and part of the vas deferens are removed.

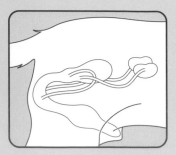

Bringing up a litter of puppies is expensive, time-consuming and messy work, so rather than risk an unwanted pregnancy, have your pet neutered.

Contraception

It is possible to administer a hormone treatment to bitches to prevent unwanted pregnancies, but there are drawbacks to prolonged birth-control treatment and vets do not like to prescribe this since it can have serious side-effects such as the development of pyometra (a life-threatening infection of the uterus) and it is not 100 per cent effective. Contraceptive drugs can also be used to prevent an unwanted pregnancy if mating has taken place (misalliance) – rather like the human 'morning after' pill.

Chemical castration (comprising an anti-testosterone drug administered by injection) is available for males, but again is not totally effective and dogs can, and will, still mate bitches. Side-effects include an increased appetite and a change in hair colour at the site of the injection. Surgical neutering remains the best option to prevent conception.

Neuter policy

Many of the bigger rescue organisations neuter all their animals as a matter of course. Usually, this is because they see, at first hand, the tragedy of too many pets for too few good homes. Neutering ensures that reproduction stops with the dogs that go through their hands.

Frequently asked question

Q I've heard that it is best to let a bitch have a litter before she is neutered. Is this true?

A This popular myth is based on human needs rather than scientific fact, as there is no evidence to suggest that it is necessary. If you want to raise a litter and are confident that you can then place the resulting puppies in good homes, a bitch can be spayed after weaning to prevent further pregnancies.

Top tip

After neutering, keep the dog on the lead during post-opeative exercise for around 2 weeks. After this, most male dogs can return to normal exercise and bitches can do so more gradually, but discourage jumping and leaping for another 4–8 weeks.

Reproduction

Species survival depends upon procreation, and pregnancy and birth are the most natural things in the world. In unneutered dogs, the urge to reproduce and pass genes on to the next generation is very strong, and a healthy bitch with access to males and a plentiful food supply can produce two litters of puppies a year. See the checklist for things to ensure before breeding a litter.

Checklist

✔ the parents are good examples of their breed and are sound and healthy
✔ the blood lines are free from defects
✔ good homes can be found for the puppies
✔ the bitch is mature enough to breed from – usually the second or third season is soon enough, depending on the breed
✔ you have suitable facilities for whelping and in which to keep the puppies until they are ready to go to new homes

Sexual maturity

Bitches only mate when they are 'in season' (also known as 'on heat'). They only have one oestrus in each breeding season (usually twice a year and lasting for around 21 days), during which they will accept a mating; this time occurs 10–14 days into the season, once her vaginal discharge turns from bloody to clear. This is unique as far as we know in the animal kingdom, and it means that there are only a few days in each season when the bitch can conceive.

A male, on the other hand, is always ready for mating when sexually mature. He will normally be indifferent to a bitch that is not in season, but will be attracted to her when her body releases the chemicals known as pheromones indicating her sexual condition. This happens a few days before she becomes sexually receptive, which explains why male dogs are so excited by bitches who are not yet ready to receive their advances and who may repulse them fiercely.

Most bitches reach puberty at about 6–7 months of age, but some may do so as early as 4 months, while others may not have their first season until they are 2 years old. Bitches should not be bred from before they are a year old, as they are not mature enough physically; it is preferable to wait until they are 18 months old before mating them for the first time. If a potential breeding bitch has not had a season by the time she is 2 years old, seek veterinary advice.

When the bitch is ready to mate, she will stand quite still with her tail held to one side. The dog mounts her from the rear and mates.

While mating, the pair may remain 'tied' (known as the copulatory tie or lock) together like this for up to 30 minutes. This is a result of the bitch's vaginal muscles closing firmly around the dog's penis so he is unable to 'escape'. Although this is not essential to a successful mating, a tie prevents sperm-bearing fluid from escaping, thus enhancing the chances of the bitch conceiving. Do not forcibly separate the dogs during a tie as this will cause them pain and possibly injury.

Looking after the pregnant bitch

Apart from increasing her diet with food specially formulated for expectant bitches to cope with the demands being made on her body, treat the mother as normal during pregnancy. As she becomes larger, she will slow down and become more reluctant to race around. Do not encourage her to jump about and run after toys. If she becomes constipated (a side-effect of pregnancy), substitute one of her daily meals with oily food such as pilchards or sardines, as this will aid the passing of motions.

Prepare a whelping site or box and place it in a quiet and undisturbed area of the house. Line the base with newspaper for insulation and place a thick layer of paper towels or washable 'vet bed' fleece on top to make a soft, absorbent mattress for the birth. Show the bitch where the 'nest' is, although bear in mind that she may ultimately choose her own preferred place.

With longhaired bitches, clip hair surrounding the birth canal (to aid hygiene and ease of delivery) and nipples (to facilitate ease of suckling). Sponge her anal area twice a day if she is carrying a large litter and is unable to do this herself. Make sure she is free of fleas and worms before and after birth – consult your vet regarding suitable treatment.

Labour and birth

Females give birth and raise their young following instinctive behaviour patterns that allow them to do so unaided, although they do get better at this with practice. Labour and birth normally proceed easily. Once second-stage labour begins (when the bitch goes into the whelping area or box and lies down), puppies are normally born around 20–60 minutes apart. Breeds with large heads, such as Bulldogs, generally need help to give birth, by Caesarean section, as they cannot do so naturally.

If you suspect that all is not well during whelping, with the bitch straining for longer than 60 minutes without a result, contact your vet immediately as she may need help. Puppies should arrive head first; the hindquarters coming out first (breech presentation) could indicate a problem.

Did you know ...?

If the puppies are unwanted, and you cannot place them with a charity, then veterinary euthanasia is the most humane and legal method of disposing of them. Consult your vet or local animal charity.

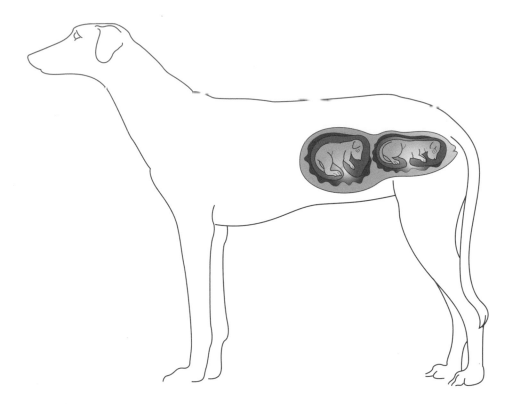

As second stage labour begins, uterine contractions move the pupies down the birth canal (vagina).

The miracle of birth

The gestation period in canines is 9 weeks (approximately 63 days). Movement of the foetuses can be felt from the seventh week of pregnancy.

As the birth nears, the bitch will begin to 'nest' and seek a private, preferably dark, safe place in which to give birth.

Once first-stage labour starts, the bitch will pace around restlessly, whining or panting, and look behind her in an agitated and puzzled manner. There will usually be a clear or mucus-like discharge from the vulva and the bitch will spend a good deal of time licking and cleaning herself. She will normally refuse food. The first stage can last for 24–48 hours.

As second-stage labour begins, the bitch goes to her nesting place, lies on her side and strains as uterine contractions move the puppies, one at a time, down the birth canal.

After delivering a puppy, the bitch cleans away the birth membranes covering it, thus allowing and stimulating it to breathe. The placenta, joined to the puppy by the umbilical cord, is then passed, and the bitch eats it, severing the cord a short way from the puppy's body.

Once all the puppies are born, the bitch will clean herself, then settle down to suckle her babies, curling herself around them, and rest. If she will go outside to relieve herself, it will give you the chance to remove soiled bedding, and also to check visually that all the pups seem healthy and content (it is wise not to handle them for the first 2–3 days, particularly if it is the bitch's first litter).

Birth problems

Occasionally, things do go wrong. If the bitch has been straining hard for over an hour without results, call out a vet immediately to help her give birth. Sometimes, for various reasons, puppies do not survive. If the bereaved bitch appears distressed, contact your vet for advice: the bitch may require medication to suppress her milk and help to prevent potential mastitis, or her loss may have a happy ending if the vet knows of orphaned puppies needing a foster mum. Other problems that can arise during pregnancy or following birth include the following (consult your vet immediately if any of these instances occur):

• Miscarriage due either to illness or because the foetuses are not healthy

• Uterine infection after birth, indicated by high fever, vomiting, lack of appetite, and dark-coloured, often smelly, vaginal discharge

Newborn puppies' eyes are sealed shut and begin to open at about 10–14 days old. A puppy cannot see with clarity or accuracy until it is about 4 weeks old, but at 15 days old its ears are open and fully functional. Milk teeth begin to appear when the pups are about 14 days old. Young puppies should be wormed under veterinary advice, while still nursing if necessary.

• Prolapsed uterus indicated by a swollen red mass appearing out of the vulva

Mother care

During whelping, offer the bitch small drinks of water and glucose. Following birth, she will probably be extremely hungry and appreciate a light meal of egg and milk, or a meat and cereal broth. The bitch will eat and drink more than normal to maintain a plentiful milk supply. Increase her food intake to around three times her usual amount, split into 3–4 meals a day. Her diet needs to be rich in calcium, protein, vitamins and minerals to sustain her

Frequently asked question

Q A friend's bitch died of eclampsia and she had to raise the puppies herself. What is this condition, and what should I do if my pregnant bitch gets it?

A Also known as milk fever or lactation tetany, eclampsia is the paralysis of milk production in the dam's teats after whelping. It is usually due to a calcium deficiency in the diet, and can occur up to 21 days after whelping. Occasionally it can occur just prior to whelping. Symptoms of eclampsia include profuse salivation, anxiety, aversion to light, lack of co-ordination, high temperature and convulsions. If the condition is not quickly treated with calcium and glucose injections, the bitch will die.

body's needs while lactating, plus she needs a constant and plentiful supply of fresh, clean water to ensure she produces enough milk.

Weaning

At 3–4 weeks, the puppies start to explore outside of the nest, and experiment with lapping at liquid foods (milk and cereal baby foods are best), and progressing at 4–5 weeks on to more solid nourishment – choose food specially formulated for puppies to make sure they receive the nutrients their rapidly growing bodies need. To encourage the puppies to start eating solids, start with a saucer of tepid milk – wipe some around their muzzles with your finger, or gently dip their noses into it, to start them off lapping at it. Sometimes it can take several attempts, but they get there in the end, so don't force the puppies – if they don't want it, try again the following day. Once they are lapping at the milk, then add cereal to it – leaving it to soak and soften before giving it to the pups. Then progress onto meat-based puppy food. Feed the puppies from shallow bowls so that they can get at the food easily. As they eat increasing amounts of solids, their excreta changes and their mother stops cleaning up after them – so now it is time to put newspaper down on the floor so you can easily clean up their excreta.

Bitches naturally wean their puppies themselves as their milk gradually dries up 5–6 weeks after the birth. At this age, the puppies should be fully weaned on to solid puppy food, although they may still return to mum for the occasional comfort suckle if allowed. By 8 weeks, the puppies are usually fully independent of their mother regarding food and hygiene requirements, and are ready for rehoming. For puppy care from 8 weeks onwards, see pages 94–97.

Mastitis

Some bitches may suffer from mastitis due to a bacterial infection. Symptoms of this include hard, hot teats that produce bloodstained or abnormal-looking milk. The affected bitch will be off colour, and may vomit and have little or no appetite. Seek veterinary attention immediately so that the bitch can be appropriately treated, and you can be shown how to hand-strip her teats and hand-rear puppies if necessary. If promptly treated, most cases of mastitis clear up within 36–48 hours.

Orphaned puppies

In the rare instances when unweaned puppies are abandoned or orphaned, it is necessary to hand-rear them. If the puppies are left without a mother for any reason, consult your vet immediately – they may know of a potential canine foster mother, be able to put you in touch with an experienced breeder for tips, or offer advice themselves on how to hand-rear the puppies.

When hand-rearing, puppies need feeding every 2 hours for the first week.

Canine fact

Although the mother can sometimes appear to be quite rough with her babies, even making them squeal, when playing with them and teaching them to fight, she is not really hurting them, so this is nothing to be alarmed about.

Top tip

A large puppy pen, in which to put the pups for brief periods when weaning begins, will provide the mother with periods of much-needed rest. You can also encourage puppies to soil in one designated place by placing a small amount of their faeces in a low-sided large cat-litter tray containing newspaper – sometimes this works, and sometimes it doesn't. If it does, it can of course make house training easier.

The more puppies are positively handled by adults and children, including humans unfamiliar to them, the more sociable they will be.

Stages of growth

Newborn

Puppies are totally dependent on their mother and her milk for the first 3 weeks. After this, they begin to experiment with eating the solid food that their dam brings back in the form of prey for them to eat, or that their human carer provides. Keeping her puppies clean is a vital role for the mother, whose babies might otherwise die of disease. The mother continues to wash them all over until the babies learn how to do this themselves; she also prompts them to relieve themselves by licking their genitals.

2–3 weeks

Begin to handle the puppies from 2 weeks old to start the vital canine-human socialization process. At this age, the mother will not be too anxious about familiar humans touching her babies. During this period, the puppy's teeth begin to appear and he will learn to walk and lap liquid puppy food such as milk and porridge. He also develops the ability to urinate and defecate unaided by his mother, and his senses of smell and hearing begin to operate.

4–5 weeks

By now, the mother will begin to discipline her puppies with a growl, usually to prevent them feeding at will. By the age of 4 weeks, puppies can see more clearly and they can stand quite well and toddle around on short, unsteady legs. At this stage they can roll over and right themselves, and play with their siblings with paw pats, bared teeth, growling and play-bites – they will also carry objects in their mouth. Their senses are more efficient, they wag their tails and begin to attempt barking.

By the end of the 4th week, the puppies are curious about their environment, can move around confidently and can often run and balance well by the end of the 5th week. However, it will be another 5–6 weeks before they can run, jump and leap with accuracy, balance and co-ordination. By this time, they will be eating more solid puppy food and should be handled and gently played with on a regular basis from now on. Puppies will now be leaving the sleeping area to relieve themselves.

6 weeks

Facial and ear expressiveness are evident and the puppy has full use of his eyes and ears. Dominance and hierarchy games will be seen among litter mates. Weaning on to puppy foods proper can now been introduced as he will no longer be totally dependent on his mother's milk and, as his milk teeth are as sharp as needles, she will be reducing the amount of time she feeds the pups (see page 44 for feeding guidance and the daily amount of food required). First vaccinations can be done.

7–19 weeks

Second vaccinations can be done at 10 weeks. Puppies are usually by now fully weaned and well socialized with humans, and preferably other animals too, and are ready to go to new homes for their obedience and socialization training to continue. House training should begin, as should name and lead training.

Juvenile (12 weeks to 6 months)

Puppies are eager to please their owners. Chewing and mouthing behaviour is common as the puppy is teething, so he should be given appropriate toys on which to do so. He should also learn to inhibit play-biting behaviour with humans and it should not be encouraged. At this stage he should learn his place in the human family, that is the bottom of the pack, otherwise he may try to exert dominance over them. Manners and obedience training should be done on a regular basis – the older the puppy gets, the better his concentration and ability to learn will become.

Adolescent (6–18 months)

During this period, the puppy becomes much more independent and is likely to challenge authority. Sexual maturity is reached; bitches come into season, with associated behavioural changes, and males experience dramatic fluctuations in male hormone levels. Territorial behaviour begins to develop. This is the most difficult time for owners to live through, and the time when many people give up their dogs for rehoming. If you have laid down solid foundations of good behaviour up to this point, adolescence will be less wearing for all concerned.

Adult (18 months and over)

The dog will now be physically mature, albeit with some filling out to do. His character is fully formed although some refinements will still be occurring. Young adults continue to develop in character and will finally settle down at about 3 years of age. Refinement and continuation of training is needed, but if owners have done their job well, they can relax and enjoy many years with their well-balanced, sociable and obedient four-legged friend.

Did you know ...?

False pregnancies can occur in dogs. Also known as 'pseudo' or 'phantom' pregnancy, this condition is quite natural and may occur in a bitch that has failed to conceive during a season.

In some cases, the owner may not notice any difference in the female's mental or physical state, while in other bitches the false pregnancy can result in a swollen abdomen and mammary glands which may also fill with milk. In severe cases, seek veterinary advice and treatment where necessary.

In the case of the latter, the bitch may also spend time nest-building, crying and be reluctant to exercise; she may even display the pushing actions of an actual birth. Such bitches will form attachments to inanimate objects, such as toys, and some have 'invisible' puppies. Her territorial and maternal instincts will show as she protects her invisible litter, which can be upsetting for the owner.

Pseudo pregnancies are triggered by the bitch's hormone levels, and are a natural way of ensuring that, in a pack of wild dogs or wolves, there are many bitches producing milk and capable of rearing or helping to rear a litter.

Accidents and first aid

Accidents usually happen when least expected, so It is sensible to be prepared at all times. A knowledge of first aid can be useful and, in some instances, essential. Emergency situations need immediate action; if you know what to do, you may be able to limit the injuries sustained by your dog, and perhaps even save his life. When administering first aid, the actions to take are shown on the checklist.

Checklist

✔ always remember your own safety is paramount
✔ assess the situation
✔ protect yourself and others from injury
✔ examine the dog
✔ diagnose injuries
✔ treat injuries or treat for pain as appropriate
✔ keep the dog warm, calm and quiet
✔ protect the dog from further injury
✔ contact a vet for professional advice and treatment

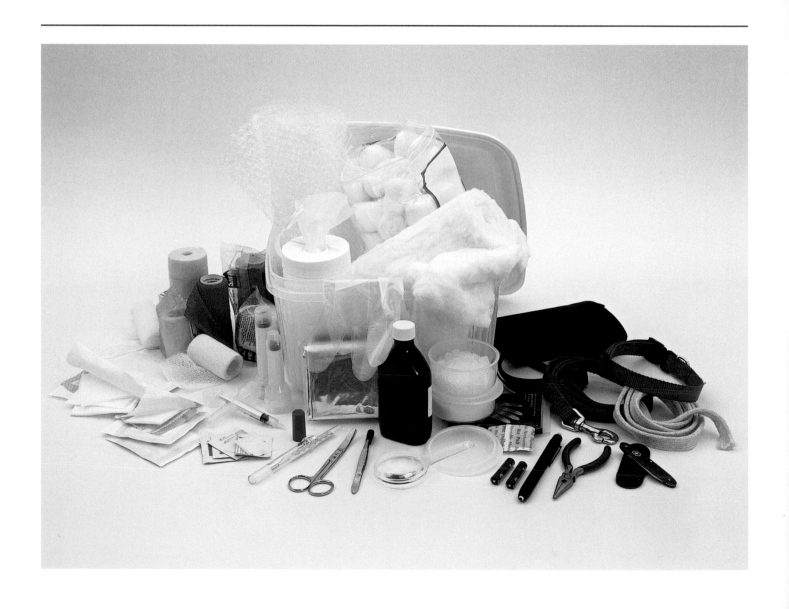

First-aid training

Having a basic training in the subject will give you the confidence to deal with an emergency situation calmly and efficiently until an expert practitioner can take over. Some vet clinics run courses in basic first aid, and it is well worth enlisting on one of these.

First-aid kit

Basic first-aid items can be bought from your vet, local pharmacy or good pet stores. A first-aid kit should contain the following:

absorbent paper (kitchen) roll to wipe up any liquid mess
antihistamine to ease insect stings and bites
antiseptic lotion for cleaning wounds – particularly animal bites
antiseptic wound powder for treating wounds and promoting healing
bandages to keep dressings in place
conforming ('sticky') bandage useful for holding dressings in place
cotton buds dampen and use to remove grass seeds or other foreign objects from the eyes and to clean wounds and apply ointments
cotton wool to bathe eyes and nose,

An injured or ill dog should be covered with a 'space blanket', blanket or towel to keep him warm and help alleviate shock symptoms while waiting for veterinary attention.

clean wounds and use as part of a dressing; dampen before use to prevent strands from sticking to a wound
curved, round-ended scissors to clip fur and trim dressings to size
dog nail clippers choose the guillotine variety
elizabethan collar to prevent a dog from interfering with dressings or sutures
glucose powder to make rehydrating fluid, mix 1 tablespoon of glucose with 1 teaspoon of table salt in 1 litre (2 pints) of warm water
heavy-duty protective gloves for when restraining a dog
kaolin pectate for diarrhoea; obtain it from a vet and follow their dosage instructions
KY jelly or vaseline to lubricate the thermometer before insertion into the rectum
muzzle to place on an injured dog before you inspect him – if he's frightened and/or in pain, he may bite; a basket muzzle is best
non-stick dressings useful for cuts
pencil torch and batteries to inspect the mouth and ears
rectal thermometer to ascertain

temperature – aural (which inserts in the ear) or digital thermometers are the easiest to use
round-ended tweezers to remove insect stings
small stainless steel or plastic bowls for use when bathing wounds
space blanket or large sheet of plastic 'bubble wrap' to wrap the dog in to maintain body temperature in cases of shock and hypothermia
squares of clean cotton material to place over wounds or stem blood flow
sterile eye wash contact lens saline solution can be used
sticky surgical plaster tape ('Elastoplast') to hold dressings in place
styptic pencil to stem the flow of capillary blood from minor cuts or bleeding claws and nails; application stings, so muzzle the dog first
surgical gloves for when treating wounds
surgical spirit to remove ticks
syringe plunger to administer liquid medicine
table salt to make saline solution (2 teaspoons of salt dissolved in 1 litre/2 pints of warm water) with which to clean wounds and counter infection

Top tip

A seriously injured or dangerously ill dog is better nursed at an animal hospital than at home where full facilities and veterinary skills are not available.

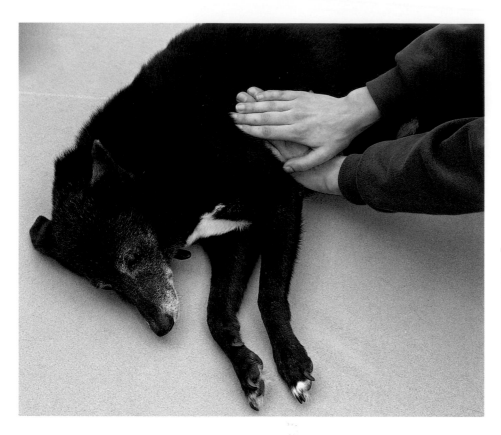

If your dog has no heartbeat, it is essential that chest compression begins as soon as possible. Never attempt chest compression, however, if you suspect the dog may have a chest injury.

Top tip

One way of checking that a dog is breathing is to place a small mirror close to his mouth and nose – if it mists and demists, then he is breathing.

First-aid basics – ABC

The basic principles of first aid are as simple as ABC – Airway, Breathing, Circulation. The priority is to make sure the dog's airway is clear to enable him to breathe and ensure blood is circulating properly (that his heart is beating). When satisfied, you can deal with any other symptoms as appropriate.

Airway and breathing

If the dog is unconscious in a collapsed state, check that he is breathing. If there is little or no breathing and the tongue is blue-black, open the mouth and remove anything blocking the airway. Gently lift the chin to extend the dog's neck to open the airway. If he still does not breathe, administer **artificial respiration**:

• Hold the mouth shut and cover the nose with your mouth.

• Gently breathe up the dog's nose – 30 breaths every minute (taking your mouth from his nose between breaths to allow for exhalation).

• With a small dog, an alternative method of artificial respiration is to hold him by his hind legs and, keeping your arms straight, swing him to the left and then to the right. This transfers the weight of the dog's internal organs on and off the diaphragm, causing the lungs to fill and empty of air. **Caution:** never try this if an injury is suspected that may be aggravated by using this method.

• Keep artificial respiration up until the dog begins to breathe on his own, veterinary help arrives or you believe the dog to be beyond help.

Circulation

Next, check for a heartbeat. Do this by putting your ear on the dog's chest on the left side, just behind his elbow,

and you will be able to hear it. Also check for a pulse – place fingers in the same position as your ear, or on the inside of the dog's thigh in the groin area (see page 91). If there is no heartbeat begin, **chest compression** as described below – the techniques vary with the size of the dog.

• For small dogs (up to the size of a Cocker Spaniel), squeeze the chest with your hands. To do this, place one hand either side of the dog's chest, just behind his elbows, and squeeze and release the chest in a smooth action, giving two compressions every second. Always use the flat of the hand, never the fingers. Don't use too much force, as it is easy to break the ribs.

• For larger dogs, place both hands on the dog's left-hand side, about level with his elbow. Apply steady pressure and release the pressure at the rate of two compressions per second.

Whichever method you choose to use, give two breaths to the dog for every four compressions. Keep this up until the dog's heart begins to beat, you can't do any more or a vet takes over. Keep checking for a heartbeat or pulse throughout your attempts at heart massage.

Moving and lifting an injured dog

Don't move an injured dog unless you have to, as any movement may aggravate his injuries. However, if it is imperative that he is moved, see page 87 for the safe lifting and carrying technique. You may need help to move a large dog safely; if you are alone, you can move a large, unconscious dog by gently and smoothly dragging or rolling him on to a coat or blanket, and carefully dragging him to safety. Muzzle him before you move him.

It is imperative to remain firm and kind while restraining and moving an injured dog. Talk quietly and calmly to the dog to soothe him. Never frighten him by using force to restrain him.

It is easier to restrain, examine or treat a dog at waist height; so, if possible, place him on a table or bench – cover this with a blanket or other material first to prevent him from slipping and panicking. Restrain him gently but firmly (by the collar if he is wearing one, or your arm around his neck if he will allow it and it won't aggravate any injury) while you assess what should be done next. Placing your hand over his back and under his chest will allow you to hold him firmly and safely while you apply appropriate first aid. To help ensure that your dog will always be fairly easy to restrain, practise restraint on him throughout his life – starting when he is a puppy.

Basic first aid

Burns and scalding

Cool the burnt area with iced water (if you can stand the dog in a bath or sink, pour cold water on the affected area for about 10 minutes) to reduce the pain and the severity of the burn. Then cover the burn lightly with a cool, damp clean cloth (handkerchief or drying-up towel), wrap the dog in a space blanket (or equivalent) and take him to the vet for expert treatment.

Chemical burns

To prevent the dog licking the affected area, put a muzzle on him. Put rubber gloves on and wash the affected area under cold running water – either by standing the dog in the bath or sink and running water over the burn, or using a hosepipe in the garden. Follow the instructions as for burns and scalds.

Sunburn

Treat as for burns and scalds.

Poisoning

If you suspect that your dog has ingested a poisonous substance (profuse salivating is the most obvious sign, while sleepiness can indicate ingestion of rat poison), contact your vet immediately and tell them what has happened. This will allow the practice time to get relevant information from the poison manufacturer while you are getting your dog to the surgery.

If you are instructed by the vet to make your dog vomit, in order to rid its digestive system of the poison as much as possible, place a couple of washing soda (sodium carbonate) crystals on the back of the dog's tongue. Alternatively, use mustard or salt mixed with a little water. Get the dog to the veterinary clinic swiftly.

Broken bones

Signs of fractured bones – apart from them protruding from the skin – include extreme pain on moving a limb, swelling, tenderness, loss of control and/or deformity of the limb, unnatural movement of the limb, or the sensation (or sound) of the two ends of the bone grinding against each other (crepitus). Keep the dog as still, quiet and warm as possible and contact your veterinary clinic to ask what to do in the circumstances.

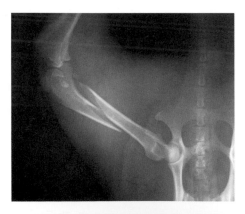

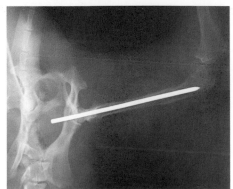

Top: an X-ray of a fractured femur before treatment. Bottom: a pin has been inserted down the centre of the femur to strengthen and support it until it heals.

Road accidents

• If the dog has been involved in a road accident and is still in the road, stop the traffic so that you can safely recover him and/or administer first aid as appropriate. Seek veterinary attention as soon as possible, informing the vet of any signs or symptoms of injury you have spotted.

• Approach the dog carefully. Speak softly and reassuringly to him to help soothe him and keep him calm and, if it is safe to do so, examine him to assess injuries and, if necessary, whether you can move him without worsening his condition. Try not to aggravate any injuries when picking him up and moving him; the best way to do so is to slide a board under him as a makeshift stretcher. As well as checking for obvious signs of injury, inspect the back of the neck for lumps and swellings that may indicate broken bones or trauma swellings.

• Having administered appropriate first aid, keep the dog warm and soothe him until expert help arrives. Even if the dog appears to have suffered no external injury, a thorough veterinary check-up is essential in case there is unseen internal haemorrhaging which could be life-threatening if not detected and treated.

Supporting the injured limb with bandages and a splint is preferable, but this should only be attempted by a calm and competent first aider.

Electrocution (electric shock)

Once the power supply has been turned off, check that the dog is breathing – if not, begin artificial respiration (see page 158). If it is not possible to switch off the power

supply, don't approach the dog. Electrocution will almost inevitably cause burns, which will need treating as described above.

Insect stings and bites

A dog will usually yelp and frantically paw at the area of his body where he has been stung. If the dog has been stung in the throat, seek veterinary attention immediately, as swelling may quickly block the airways and kill the dog.

For stings elsewhere on the body, clip the fur from around the affected area so you can see what the problem is. Wash it with saline solution: bees leave their sting in the victim, wasps do not. If you can see the sting and judge it is removable with tweezers, then do so, and then wipe the area with cotton wool dampened with surgical spirit. To neutralize the effect of a wasp sting, wipe the area with vinegar; use bicarbonate of soda for bee stings. Then dry the area thoroughly, but gently, and apply a wet compress to help reduce the irritation and swelling. For other insect bites, clean and dry the area, and apply antihistamine spray or ointment to reduce itching and irritation.

Bite wounds

Dogs are at risk from three main types of animal bite – dog, rat and snake.

• For dog bites, clip the fur away from around the bite and clean the wound thoroughly with saline solution, followed by diluted antiseptic lotion. Dry the area, and then apply a liberal dusting of antiseptic wound powder. Repeat twice daily – keep the wound clean or it may fester, become infected and result in an abscess.

• Rat bites are especially dangerous, as these rodents carry many harmful diseases. Treat immediately as for dog bites, and then take your pet to a vet who may administer an antibiotic injection and prescribe an antibiotic dusting powder for the wound.

• Keep dogs bitten by a snake as calm as possible and prevent them from running around, or even making any

movements, as this will speed up the circulation of the venom around the body. Seek immediate veterinary attention.

Drowning

Once the dog has been pulled from the water, hold him upside down (or lift his back end up if a large dog) to drain the water from his lungs. Then lay him flat and rub his body fairly vigorously to promote respiration. If he is not breathing, commence artificial respiration (see page 158) and summon veterinary help as soon as possible.

Foreign bodies

Most foreign bodies lodged in an area of the body are best left to a vet to remove – contact your veterinary clinic for advice. If the dog is pawing at the affected area, gently restrain him to prevent further damage occurring until your vet takes over and deals with it. Grass seeds can sometimes be flushed out of the eye using a syringe filled with saline solution, while thorns can often be extracted from paws fairly easily – but check that the end has not broken off and been left in the wound. If this happens, seek veterinary treatment, otherwise it may fester.

Choking

Choking warrants immediate action: take a secure hold of the dog and open his mouth to see if there is anything stuck in his throat. The main worry is that, in trying to remove a foreign object, you will push it further down the throat and make matters worse. If you have a helper, ask them to hold his mouth open while you remove the blockage.

Many instances of choking are caused by bits of branches (which owners have thrown for their dogs to fetch) blocking the airway. Never throw sticks for your dog – choose appropriate toys instead (see page 32).

If whatever is blocking the airway is wedged in place, don't try to pull it or you may cause more damage; instead, sit down, hold the dog's hind legs, lift them over and hold them between your knees. Place one hand either side of the chest and squeeze using jerky movements, making the dog 'cough'. Squeeze about 5–6 times, and the dog should cough out the object. Let your dog rest, and then take him for a veterinary check-up. If the object does not come out, take the dog to the vet immediately.

Fits and convulsions

Do not hold down a fitting dog – take away any objects around him that he could harm himself on, and seek veterinary attention urgently. Seizures are extremely serious and potentially life-threatening.

A dog is lame if he is incapable of normal locomotion, or moving with an abnormal gait.

Lameness

If your dog suddenly becomes lame, is unable to bear his weight on one or more of his legs, or cannot walk, check for foreign objects lodged in a limb or paw and also for broken bones. Keep him still until a vet can examine him.

Shock

Shock comprises an acute fall in blood pressure following an accident, injury, illness or terrifying experience, and is life-threatening. Signs of shock include: cool skin, pale lips and gums (due to a lack of blood circulation); faint, rapid pulse; staring but unseeing eyes. Keep the dog quiet and warm by wrapping him in a space blanket (or equivalent) and promote blood circulation by gently but firmly massaging his body, taking care not to aggravate any injuries in doing so. Seek veterinary attention as soon as possible.

Bleeding wounds

Most cuts and lacerations heal on their own fairly quickly; keep them clean with cotton wool dampened with saline solution. Initial bleeding, which may be profuse, helps clean the wound of debris, lessening the possibility of infection. Seek veterinary attention immediately, however, if:

• the wound is spouting bright red (arterial) blood in jets
• a constant flow of dark red (venous) blood refuses to cease
• the wound is deep or serious enough to cause concern, as sutures may be required
• gunshot wounds are suspected
• the skin has been punctured – these wounds appear tiny on the surface, but can be quite deep and are, therefore, particularly prone to becoming infected. Never attempt to remove a foreign object from such a wound as this may aggravate the injury and/or allow large amounts of bleeding to occur (while it is in place, the object acts as a plug and may be preventing massive blood loss)
• cuts affect toes or a limb as tendon damage may have occurred

In the case of minor wounds, blood flow can be stemmed by gentle direct pressure using a dampened clean pad of cotton material, before cleaning them. Where arterial or venous bleeding is present, apply indirect pressure (not on the wound itself) to the appropriate artery or vein if you can feel it on the heart side of the wound; otherwise press a cotton pad over the wound to help stem the flow of blood. Elevating the injury, if possible, will enable gravity to help reduce the blood flow.

Internal injuries

These can be detected by swelling of the abdomen, bleeding from the mouth, nose, ears, eyes, sex organs (not to be confused with a bitch's oestrus) or anus; bloodstained urine and/or stools, shock and signs of bruising on the skin. Seek veterinary attention immediately.

Frequently asked question

Q How loose or tight should bandages be?

A If you have not done a veterinary first-aid course, bandaging is best left to vets and veterinary nurses, since incorrect application can do more harm than good by restricting blood circulation. Ask your local vet clinic to show you what different bandages are used for and how to apply them correctly.

Top tip

To clip fur around wounds, use a pair of scissors with curved blades and rounded ends. Dip the blades in clean, preferably boiled and cooled water, and then carefully clip the fur around the wound; the fur will stick to the wet blades, preventing it from falling into the wound. Dip the scissors in the water again to swill off the clippings.

DON'T MAKE IT WORSE!

SITUATION	WHAT NOT TO DO
Wounds	DON'T apply direct pressure to a wound with an object impaled in it, or with bone protruding from it, or attempt to remove any objects from wounds, since this may aggravate massive blood loss; leave this to a vet.
Severe bleeding	DON'T apply a tourniquet, since it can cut off the blood flow completely, causing severe – often life-threatening – danger to the dog.
Chest compression	DON'T attempt chest compression if a chest injury is suspected.
Choking	DON'T attempt to remove an object wedged in the mouth or throat, other than by the coughing method described on page 161. If this fails, leave it to a vet.
Burns	DON'T apply too much cold water at once to the affected area since too sudden a drop in temperature may cause more disastrous problems. See page 159.
Electrocution	DON'T touch the dog without switching off the power supply first to prevent you too from being electrocuted.
Chemical burns	DON'T attempt to treat the dog without first putting on gloves and protective clothing to prevent the chemicals burning you.
Fits and convulsions	DON'T attempt to hold down a fitting dog.
Fractures	DON'T try to splint a broken bone – leave this to a vet.
Poisoning	DON'T make the dog vomit unless the vet gives specific guidelines to do so.
Fights	DON'T try to break up a dog fight using your hands – use a long broom handle, a bucket of cold water or a gushing hose pipe to separate the dogs and give you the opportunity to control them.
Eye injuries	DON'T apply a bandage or compress to an eye if you suspect there may be a foreign body in it.
Ingested string	DON'T try to pull foreign bodies from the mouth or anus if you meet with resistance in doing so – seek veterinary attention instead.

Common ailments

Dogs can suffer from a range of illnesses, many of which can be treated successfully. To give your dog the best chance of recovery, you must seek veterinary advice and treatment quickly, and faithfully follow all instructions given regarding medication and care. The vet will be able to treat your dog more effectively if you can provide as many details as possible about him – and this is where knowing your dog well can be, quite literally in some cases, a lifesaver. Details to provide your vet with are shown on the checklist.

Checklist

✓ your pet's symptoms
✓ when they started
✓ how long they have been present
✓ how your dog's usual behaviour is affected

Blindness or impaired vision

There are degrees of impaired vision; the term 'blind' is usually only used when the dog can see nothing at all, or perhaps just light and dark.

Symptoms
Your dog may bump into furniture and objects for no apparent reason, or have difficulty finding you – especially if you are in a group of people. It is also quite common for an elderly dog to have more problems with his eyesight in bright light and in darkness, and he may be reluctant to venture out at such times.

Causes
A variety – from injury to hereditary diseases and conditions. As dogs age, it is quite common for a bluish colour to appear in the eyes as the lens of the eye deteriorates.

What to do
Any dog showing symptoms of failing eyesight should be taken to a vet without delay.

Treatment
This depends upon the cause, but many cases of total blindness are untreatable.

Cloudy or opaque eyes indicate a sight problem (blindness); many dogs adjust remarkably well to being blind in one or both eyes.

Abnormal tear production

This is also called epiphora. Tears flush dirt and debris from the eyes, working together with the eyelids, and so play an important role in keeping the eyes healthy.

Symptoms

Tears overflow onto the face; it is most obvious in white-faced dogs. Toy breeds are susceptible to the condition, as are those with large, droopy eyelids.

Causes

One or both tear ducts being blocked due to a foreign body, an infection, facial injury, scarring following an injury or excessive mucus production. The tear ducts may be unable to function correctly due to a congenital defect (one present from birth). Irritation of the eye due to ingrowing eyelashes can also cause epiphora.

What to do

Seek veterinary attention and advice.

Treatment

Antibiotics will be prescribed to clear up an infection, while blocked tear ducts may be washed out under anaesthetic. Prevention is better than cure, so clean your dog's eyes regularly with tepid water to remove debris from the area before it becomes a problem. This is particularly important if the dog is of a breed susceptible to this condition.

Periodontal disease

This is a disease of the gums and/or the teeth.

Symptoms

Bad breath (halitosis), swollen and tender gums, loss of appetite and excessive drooling. Plaque (a sticky film on teeth made up of food deposits mixed with saliva in which bacteria proliferate) and calculus (a build-up of minerals – also called tartar) on a dog's teeth can lead to heart and kidney disease if left untreated. Yellow-brown stains on the teeth where they meet the gums are a classic symptom.

Causes

Gingivitis (inflammation of the gums); decayed teeth; broken teeth. Halitosis is also one of the symptoms of renal failure.

What to do

Keep the dog's teeth in good condition. Regularly cleaning them can act as a preventative measure, and also as a way of inspecting the teeth and finding small problems while they can still be dealt with. Take your dog for a regular oral check-up.

Treatment

If your dog suffers from gingivitis, then it may be helpful to use an antiseptic spray in his mouth. Ask the vet for advice on this. Feeding mainly soft, canned food may adversely affect the teeth, so provide some crunchy food (kibble or biscuit-type feed) at every mealtime as this will help clean teeth. Canine 'dental toys' may also help to clean teeth, as will raw meaty bones (bare bones provide no benefit and may even damage the teeth). Don't throw stones for your dog to retrieve, as these will damage teeth.

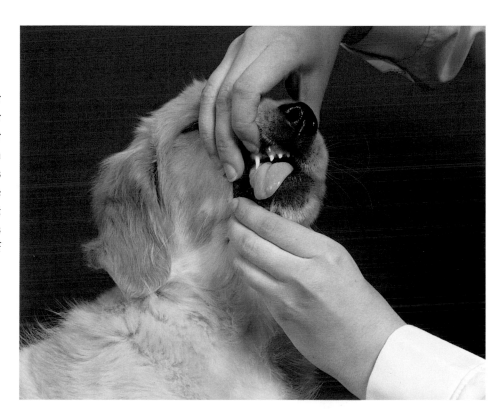

A build-up of tartar contributes to decayed teeth and gum disease.

Urinary incontinence

Urinary incontinence, the inability to control urination, is more common in bitches than dogs, particularly bitches that have been spayed.

Symptoms

If a bitch has 'accidents', particularly while lying down or sleeping, urinary incontinence is the likely cause. If a dog (male or female) dribbles urine when excited or exercising, this is likely to be a behavioural problem.

Causes

Possible causes of urinary incontinence may include faulty urethral valves, congenital defects of the dog's urinary system, urolithiasis (crystals or 'stones' of insoluble calcium in the urinary system), cancer or prostate problems (in male dogs). Urinary incontinence is seen particularly in older breeding bitches, along with medium-sized and large bitches.

What to do

When taking your dog for a veterinary examination, provide a fresh sample of his urine for testing; this will reveal if any diseases are causing the problem. It is unfair to punish or reproach a dog for incontinence. The dog's bed is likely to become soiled, so bedding must be changed and cleaned at regular and frequent intervals, preferably daily.

Treatment

Surgery may be needed to reposition an affected dog's bladder, while drug therapy may be used to improve the effectiveness of the urethra in sealing the flow of urine. Urinary incontinence is not life-threatening in

Did you know ...?

You can buy suitable beds for incontinent bitches, or easily make one from a large beanbag dog bed. Simply waterproof the bag by placing it in a heavy-duty polythene bag, cover this with several layers of newspaper and then cover the whole thing with a blanket or towel. If the dog does have an accident, simply dispose of the newspaper and wash the blanket.

itself, but as some of the possible underlying causes may be serious it is better to seek veterinary advice sooner rather than later.

Anal sac disease

This is an infection of the anal sacs. These sacs secrete an oily liquid, light brown in colour, that is expressed through two tubes as faeces pass through the anus. It is thought that this liquid is used as a means of recognition between packs and even individual dogs, and amounts of it are deposited along with every piece of faeces passed by the dog.

Symptoms

Excessive licking of the anus; yelping on defecation; nibbling at the flanks; dragging the back end along the ground which is known as 'scooting' (see page 70); obvious swellings at the site of the anal sacs; blood, pus and foul-smelling brown liquid in the anal area where badly infected anal sacs have ulcerated and burst.

Causes

When the liquid in the anal sacs thickens, which may be due to infection, it is more difficult to express normally and this leads to the sacs overfilling. If the dog starts producing the liquid at a faster rate, or the muscle tone around the anus alters, this can also lead to overfilling. The liquid in the overfilled sac then becomes impacted and the sacs may become infected, causing the dog distress and pain.

What to do

If your dog displays any of the symptoms listed above, take him to a vet; if there is discharge from the anal sacs, seek immediate attention.

Treatment

The vet will manually empty overfilled sacs, which will instantly ease the dog's discomfort. If, however, they are infected, the dog may have to be given a general anaesthetic and have his sacs flushed out; this will be followed by a course of antibiotics.

Flatulence

Gas is emitted from a dog's anus (often referred to as 'passing wind').

Symptoms

An unpleasant smell around the dog, often combined with a noise.

Causes

Poor-quality food that your dog is unable to digest properly; the dog bolting his food, thereby swallowing air with it; serious digestive disorders; eating unsuitable table scraps.

What to do

Try changing the dog's brand of food; if it was of poor quality, try him on a better-quality diet. If he is a greedy feeder, place large, smooth and clean stones in the food bowl so he has to carefully pick out the food – this will slow him down. If these actions fail, consult your vet, as a thorough examination may be needed to check there is no serious underlying cause.

Treatment

Normally flatulence can be cured by changing the dog's diet, or by avoiding feeding him the food(s) that cause the problem.

Contagious respiratory disease ('kennel cough')

This is a highly contagious disease.

Symptoms

A bad cough that worsens during exertion or when the dog pulls against the leash. Coughing bouts may end in retching or gagging and sometimes mucus is produced. There may be nasal discharge and an accompanying fever. (Other conditions that produce similar symptoms include heart worms and chronic bronchial disease.)

Causes

A type of bacterium (*Bordetella bronchiseptica*) which can also affect cats, and canine parainfluenza virus, either separately or together.

What to do

Keep the affected dog isolated from others. The condition normally clears up within a few days and the dog should make a complete recovery within 10–14 days. If the symptoms persist, contact your vet for advice, as a badly affected dog may suffer lung damage if untreated.

Treatment

Antibiotics.

Diabetes mellitus (sugar diabetes)

In this hormonal condition, the dog is unable to control his blood-sugar levels.

Symptoms

Increased appetite and thirst – particularly if coupled with other symptoms such as an increase in the amount of urine passed, lethargy, weight loss and maybe cataracts. Very often, symptoms of diabetes mellitus are seen in bitches just after they have started oestrus.

Causes

A lack of insulin (produced by the pancreas) or an increase in blood-sugar levels (hyperglycaemia). The condition may indicate that the

If your dog is going into boarding kennels, he must be vaccinated against kennel cough.

pancreas is not producing enough insulin, due to an abnormality or natural ageing. In some breeds (including German Shepherd Dog, Labrador Retriever, Rottweiler and Samoyed) the condition is thought to be hereditary. It can, however, occur in any dog, most commonly those over 8 years old. Due to the increased levels of progesterone (a hormone) in the blood during phantom or pseudo-pregnancies, unspayed bitches are said to be more than three times more susceptible to diabetes mellitus, and obese dogs of either sex are also at increased risk.

What to do

Take any dog showing symptoms of diabetes for examination by a vet.

Treatment

Treatment for this condition is likely to be long-term, as your dog may need regular insulin injections and other treatment. Treatment is usually

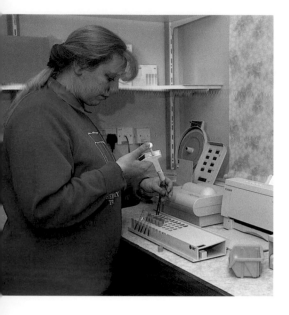

Laboratory analysis of the affected dog's urine, X-rays and ultrasound may all be required to get a full and accurate diagnosis of diabetes mellitus.

successful, providing the condition is diagnosed before it becomes chronic. Typically, you will need to collect and test a sample of urine from your dog every morning to check the glucose levels, calculate the amount of insulin needed and administer it by injection. Other possible treatments include weight loss, spaying, medication, a special diet and increased exercise.

Vomiting

This is a symptom of another condition and not an illness in itself.

Symptoms

A forceful expulsion of the contents of the dog's stomach and/or small intestine via the mouth.

Causes

These include:
- sudden change in diet
- eating unsuitable foods
- motion sickness
- heatstroke
- conditions that affect the chemical composition of the blood, such as diabetes mellitus, renal failure, liver disease or a bacterial infection
- a foreign body in the stomach
- gastric dilation/torsion
- stomach cancer
- parasitic worms
- fear and stress
- trauma to the head
- infections such as canine parvovirus or distemper
- ingestion of emetic substances, such as grass

What to do

Occasional vomiting is normal, and no action need be taken in such cases. In cases of recurring vomiting, or where large amounts of vomit are produced, or there is blood in the vomit, veterinary advice should be sought. Vomiting that you consider to be a result of your dog's scavenging, which is therefore spasmodic and not severe, is best treated by starving the dog for 24 hours. During this time, it is vital that the dog is offered regular small amounts of water to drink, to help prevent dehydration. After this time, reintroduce food with small light meals, such as scrambled eggs or boiled chicken, gradually building up to his former feeding regime. If the vomiting continues, or starts again when food is reintroduced, seek veterinary advice.

You can help prevent some of the causes of vomiting by treating your dog on a regular basis for internal parasites (worms), discouraging him from scavenging, not making sudden changes to his diet, not feeding him prior to travelling, and not overfeeding him.

Make sure the rubbish bin is inaccessible to your dog, so he can't steal leftovers from it.

Treatment

In severe cases, it is not unusual for the affected dog to be placed on an intravenous drip to keep him hydrated. Where a foreign body is wedged in the digestive system, surgery will be needed to remove it.

Diarrhoea

Like vomiting, diarrhoea is a symptom of another condition and not an illness in itself.

Symptoms

Liquid-like, pungent faeces. Greasy-looking faeces and faeces of different colours are also classed as diarrhoea, as are small amounts of normal-looking faeces that your dog passes very frequently. If your dog is suffering from colitis (an inflammation of the colon), his faeces will contain quite a lot of mucus and bright red blood. Another symptom of colitis is tenesmus, where the dog strains to defecate; this is often mistaken for a symptom of constipation.

Causes

Diarrhoea may simply be a symptom of overeating or stress. Intestinal worms are a common cause of diarrhoea, as are foreign bodies in the digestive system and fungal infections.

What to do

Prevent the dog from eating anything, but ensure that he is given adequate amounts of water. If the diarrhoea is acute, provide the dog with a rehydrating fluid (see page 157) and contact the vet. Keep your dog where you can see him and note the times of

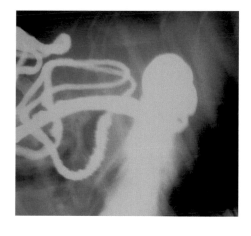

Laboratory analysis of faeces may be taken by the vet to ascertain the underlying cause of diarrhoea. Where recurrent attacks of colitis are concerned, X-rays and barium meals may be used to help determine the most effective treatment.

his motions, and also the consistency, colour and quantity of the diarrhoea. By doing this, you will help the vet to find the cause of the sudden diarrhoea, and to treat the problem effectively.

Treatment

The treatment for diarrhoea depends upon the underlying cause. If it is due to internal parasites, then anthelmintics (wormers) will be used

to rid the dog of the infestation, while antibiotics will be used for infections. Diarrhoea causes the dog to dehydrate, and can lead to irreparable body damage (particularly of the kidneys) and even death. In all cases of severe diarrhoea (where overeating is not the cause), if it persists, or if there is blood in the motions, consult the vet immediately.

Enteritis

Inflammation of the intestines results in diarrhoea.

Symptoms

Diarrhoea, often bloody.

Causes

Bacterial infection usually due to E. coli or campylobacter (in humans this type is known as dysentery).

What to do

Withhold food and seek veterinary attention immediately.

Treatment

Course(s) of antibiotics plus regular doses of kaolin.

Did you know ...?

The cause of diarrhoea may be a disease that can be transmitted to humans (zoonotic). Such diseases include campylobactor and salmonella, both caused by harmful bacteria. To reduce the chance of any of these diseases being passed on to you and your family, always wash your hands after handling your dog – and particularly before eating. Isolate the affected dog and keep him on water and electrolytes for 24 hours, dosing with kaolin solution (available from vets, doctors and pharmacies), about every 2 hours. After the fast, food intake should gradually be built up again; cooked chicken, rabbit and fish are excellent foods for a recovering dog.

It doesn't even have to be a hot day for a dog to suffer heatstroke when left in the warm confines of a car. Never leave your dog in a car for longer than 10 minutes and always leave a window slightly open to maintain a flow of fresh air.

Heatstroke

Fever is caused by the failure of the body's temperature-regulating mechanism when exposed to excessively high temperatures.

Symptoms

Agitation and extreme distress. First, the dog will stretch out and pant heavily, then drool and stagger as if drunk. Finally, if untreated, he will collapse, pass into a coma and die.

Causes

Usually due to being in a car – either on a long journey or left inside one. Inside a car, there is poor ventilation and the temperature rises to a dangerous level quickly, even in the cooler sunshine of spring or autumn. Dogs left in outside pens with no escape from the sun, or exercised on hot days, can also suffer from heatstroke, as can dogs exercised in hot weather.

What to do

You must act fast. In mildly affected dogs, simply moving them to a cool place and ensuring a steady passage of cool air will usually be sufficient for them to recover.

Treatment

In bad cases, cool the dog down with cold water from a hosepipe (fine misting spray) or by gently pouring bowlfuls over it. In very bad cases, cover the dog with wet towels, including the head (but keeping the nose and mouth clear) and keep dousing him with cold water. Seek veterinary assistance urgently. In all cases of heatstroke, it is vital to keep the head cool, as the brain may literally be cooked and brain death can occur.

Arthritis

This involves inflammation of the joints. There are two forms of arthritis that may affect dogs – osteoarthritis and traumatic arthritis.

Symptoms

Swollen joints, difficulty in walking, and lameness.

Causes

Osteoarthritis may be a condition in itself, or a result of other conditions such as hip dysplasia. It is a progressive and painful disease that will seriously affect the quality of life of the affected dog. It may affect one or more joints, and the seriousness of the condition will depend on which joints are affected, and the general health of the dog. Obese dogs are more prone to osteoarthritis.

Traumatic arthritis is caused as a direct result of an injury to the joint, for example the result of a road traffic accident or a sprain while exercising. Poor nutrition, especially in the early months of your dog's life, is another cause of the condition. It may also occur as a result of poor husbandry or old age, or be hereditary.

What to do

Your vet will advise you as to what action you should take, as this will depend on the underlying causes and treatment being given. Careful exercise routines detailed by the vet

A physical examination and observation of the dog's movement, along with X-rays and analysis of joint fluid, will give the vet an indication of how serious an arthritic problem is.

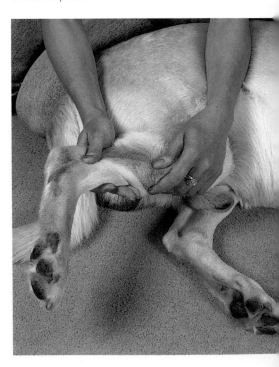

will prove beneficial in many cases. Swimming is good, as it exercises the dog's muscles without putting pressure on affected joints.

Treatment

The treatment for arthritis may include anti-inflammatory drugs and painkillers, and in some cases surgery may be needed. All cases of osteoarthritis should be treated seriously. Don't wait until your dog can't walk before consulting the vet.

Sarcoptic mange

This common, highly infectious, unpleasant, zoonotic skin condition can result in alopecia (hair loss).

Symptoms

Persistent scratching leading to red, sore skin and progressive bald patches and open sores.

Causes

The insect ectoparasite *Sarcoptes scabiei*. Dogs can become infected with this through coming into contact with other infected animals such as rodents, or simply by being on infected ground.

What to do

Seek veterinary advice and treatment. Mange can be contracted by humans (scabies). Use disposable gloves and wash your hands after handling any infected dog.

Treatment

Apply a prescribed wash that kills parasites to the affected areas. Ask your vet how best to treat your dog's bed and the areas of the house he has access to.

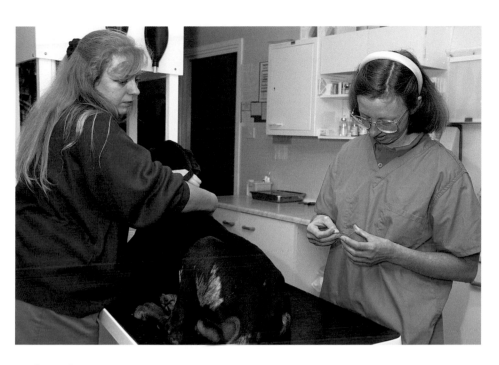

Seborrhoea

This involves abnormal or excessive secretion from the sebaceous glands.

Symptoms

Areas of dead skin that appear flaky and greasy and may be inflamed.

Causes

These are varied and can include: bacterial infection (pyoderma); food allergy; parasite infestation; incompatible coat preparations (shampoos, etc); hypothyroidism; Cushing's disease; diabetes mellitus. It may also be an inherited condition.

What to do

Seek veterinary advice to determine the cause.

Treatment

Follow prescribed treatment – this may be something as simple as changing the diet and/or brand of shampoo or coat conditioner, controlling parasites regularly, and correct grooming.

For accurate diagnosis of skin complaints, the vet will need to take non-painful 'skin scrapings' for laboratory analysis.

Alopecia

This is abnormal hair loss.

Symptoms

Loss of hair, which may be in small, localized patches, or cover large areas of the dog's body.

Causes

Stress; flea dermatitis.

What to do

Seek veterinary advice immediately to ascertain the cause of the condition (see Sarcoptic Mange above).

Treatment

Your vet will advise, as this depends on the cause. If stress is the reason, the hair usually regrows to its normal condition.

Food allergies

Dogs may develop an allergy to one or more of the contents of their feed.

Symptoms

Itchy skin; scratching – even to the point of making the skin sore.

Causes

One or more ingredients of the dog's food, the most common culprits being wheat, cow's milk and some red meats.

What to do

Try changing the diet, gradually, to one of the 'natural' commercial diets (chicken or lamb and rice often proves successful) available to see if this makes any difference. Keep the dog on the alternative diet for at least 6 weeks, as any less won't show any real change. Avoid feeding food treats containing artificial additives. Seek veterinary advice.

Treatment

Only feed a top-quality diet with no, or minimal, artificial additives.

Ringworm

This is a fungal infection of the skin.

Symptoms

Scratching and round areas of hair loss, with the visible skin becoming scaly and raised around the edge of the lesion.

Causes

Fungi, including *Microsporum canis*, *Microsporum gypseum* and *Trichophyton mentagrophytes*. Spores of these fungi may be wind-borne or found in the soil.

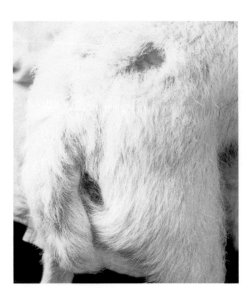

Telltale signs of ringworm infection include a round area of hair loss and scaly, flaking skin.

What to do

Some of the fungi responsible for ringworm are zoonotic (contractable by humans), so care must be taken that you and your family are not infected. Only your vet can prescribe effective treatment, so you should seek urgent advice.

Treatment

Washing the dog in fungicidal wash prescribed by a vet will help kill the fungi. Topical applications of fungicidal treatment may also be recommended.

Otitis

More commonly known as ear canker, otitis is an inflammation of the skin lining the ear and one of the most common conditions in dogs. It may occur in one or both ears.

Symptoms

These may include regular ear-scratching and head-shaking, a discharge or smell from the ear, reddening of the inner ear flap and/or the ear hole. The dog may snap at anyone who touches him even gently around the ear.

Causes

Problems occur when the ears do not get proper ventilation (such as in drop-eared breeds like Spaniels) and the wax builds up. This excess wax causes irritation, and the ear is stimulated to produce even more wax. This leads to ideal conditions for normally harmless fungi and bacteria to grow and prosper. Ear mites, foreign bodies in the ear and skin problems can also cause otitis.

What to do

Any dog showing any of the symptoms of irritated ears should be taken to the vet as soon as possible, immediately if you suspect a foreign body is lodged in the ear. *Never attempt to remove a blockage yourself, as you may damage the dog's ear permanently.* Don't put any liquid, ointment or other medication inside the dog's ears unless on the direction of your vet, nor put any solid object (including cotton buds) inside the ear, which may also damage it. Discharge from the dog's ear should not be interfered with until your vet has had a chance to see it, as this may provide some clues about the ear problem.

Treatment

This may include having the ear syringed (washed out), or the application of a topical medicine directly into the ear, such as ear drops or ointment. Whatever medications are prescribed, it is important that you administer them exactly as you are instructed and finish the course of treatment. In serious cases of recurring otitis, surgery may be necessary to improve ear ventilation. If otitis is not properly treated, it can become chronic, causing severe problems – and possibly damage to parts of the ear and the dog's hearing.

Ear mites

These insect parasites are common in dogs.

Symptoms

Persistent ear-scratching and head-shaking. A build-up of wax in the ears, dotted with black specks, is an indication that a dog may have ear mites; the black specks are probably

spots of dried blood. The mites can move down the ear canal and infect the middle ear; such an infection will cause the affected animal to lose its sense of balance. The dog may be unable to hold its head straight or, in more serious cases, may constantly fall over.

Causes

Ear mites (*Otodectes cynotis*); these mites are common in dogs, cats and wild rodents.

What to do

Seek veterinary advice in all cases of ear mites, or if your dog suffers balance loss. All animals that have been in contact with the infected dog must also be treated as ear mites can infect other animals that may not show any symptoms for some time.

Treatment

In mild cases, ear drops will be prescribed. Anti-inflammatory drugs may also be prescribed if the dog's ears are irritated. Mites are easily treated if caught early enough.

Ear drops prescribed by a vet will quickly clear up an ear-mite infection.

Canine parvovirus enteritis (parvo)

Known as 'parvovirus' or 'parvo', this causes acute gastrointestinal disease, or heart disease (parvovirus myocarditis) in young dogs.

Symptoms

General depressed demeanour with high fever, followed around 24 hours later by severe vomiting and, usually bloody, diarrhoea. This provokes a rapid decline due to dehydration which often proves fatal. If the heart is affected (usually seen in young puppies), acute distress, listlessness and sudden death (or 'fading puppy syndrome') are the most common symptoms.

Causes

A highly contagious viral infection that is shed from the mouth, nose or in the faeces of infected dogs.

What to do

You should seek veterinary attention immediately if you suspect your dog has parvo.

Treatment

There is none for the virus itself (if it attacks the heart muscle, sudden death usually occurs), but antibiotics may help prevent or reduce secondary bacterial infection. If treated early enough, the chances of survival are increased. Survivors do not generally suffer long-term detrimental effects.

Note: There is a human form of parvovirus, but this is not connected in any way to canine parvovirus enteritis, which presents no risk to human health.

Cystitis

This inflammation of the bladder can affect both males and females, but it is more common in the latter.

Symptoms

Frequent urination with only small amounts of urine passed; blood-tinged urine; severe discomfort when urinating; possibly foul-smelling, thick urine.

Causes

Bacterial infection of the bladder. Occasionally due to bladder stones.

What to do

Seek veterinary treatment.

Treatment

Antibiotics.

Mammary (breast) cancer

Breast cancer is common in unspayed bitches and almost half of mammary tumours are malignant (progressively worsening and proving fatal if untreated).

Symptoms

Lumps in a bitch's mammary glands (teats).

Causes

It is not known for sure, but is thought to be hormone-linked.

What to do

Seek veterinary attention immediately.

Treatment

The various types of treatment include:
• surgery to remove the lumps

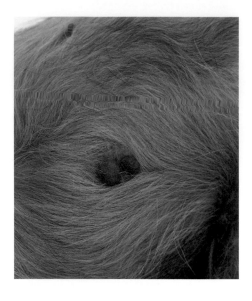

A typical mammary tumour appears as a well-defined lump on the bitch's teat.

• chemotherapy to kill or shrink the lumps
• radiotherapy to destroy diseased tissue
• hyperthermia – the application of extremely high temperatures to the tumour(s) through ultrasound or electromagnetic radiation

Unexplained lumps and bumps

Abnormal lumpy swellings of various sizes occur anywhere on the body.

Symptoms

Lumps on the skin surface, or felt under it.

Causes

There is a variety of causes, including: blocked sebaceous glands; cancerous growths; fatty deposits; abscess; an embedded thorn.

What to do

Seek veterinary attention.

Treatment

This depends on the cause. If cancer is the cause, then see 'mammary cancer' for treatment options; other causes are more easily and quickly dealt with via antibiotics or possible surgical removal.

Constipation

This is a failure to pass faeces, or a reduction in the frequency and quantity of faeces passed.

Symptoms

Extremely dry faeces and/or straining to pass faeces. A dog normally defecates 1–4 times daily; if your dog deviates from this norm, keep your eye on him for further signs that all is not well.

Causes

These include: bacterial infection; a viral infection (canine parvovirus, canine distemper); tenesmus (a form of colitis); a foreign body blocking the digestive system; a food allergy or sudden change in food; an unsuitable diet lacking in sufficient fibre; inadequate exercise; an enlarged prostrate gland in males.

What to do

If disease is suspected, the dog's condition deteriorates or he is in great discomfort, seek veterinary attention.

Treatment

Regular exercise combined with a suitable diet helps prevent many cases of constipation. If you have sought veterinary attention, due to disease, follow the prescribed treatment.

Canine distemper

This is also known as 'hard pad'.

Symptoms

Sudden high temperature, diarrhoea (sometimes yellow and bloody) and vomiting, with a cough developing and possibly sneezing and pus-like discharge from the nose. As the disease progresses, the foot pads become hard and cracked.

Causes

A virus that is spread either through direct contact or transmission through the air.

What to do

You should seek veterinary attention immediately if you suspect this disease.

Treatment

There is no cure for the virus, but clinical symptoms can be supported through antibiotics. Sufferers often do not survive; if they do, many months later they may suffer fits, bladder and bowel incontinence and/or paralysis from which they rarely recover.

Canine leptospirosis

This is a serious bacterial infection that has two forms. *Leptospirosis icterohaemorrhagiae* is contracted from contact with rats and their urine. *Leptospirosis canicola* is contracted through contact with the urine of infected dogs.

Symptoms

Any or all of these symptoms:
• *L. icterohaemorrhagiae*: high fever, dull demeanour, polydipsia, polyuria, loss of appetite, vomiting, stomach pain, heavy breathing, halitosis and mouth ulcers, vomiting and diarrhoea.
• *L. canicola*: loss of appetite, dull demeanour, jaundice, bleeding gums, diarrhoea and bright yellow urine. Death can occur within 36 hours.

Causes

Viral bacteria, as explained above.

What to do

Seek immediate veterinary attention.

Treatment

Antibiotics may help regarding *L. canicola*, but death usually occurs. Dogs that seem to recover usually develop terminal kidney failure.

Gastric dilation volvulus complex

Commonly known as GDV or 'bloat', this tends to affect large, deep-chested breeds such as German Shepherd Dogs, Rottweilers, Great Danes and Setters.

Symptoms

Restlessness, salivating, retching and depression. As the condition progresses, the stomach swells, weakness develops and the heart races. Agonizing death occurs if the condition is not treated quickly.

Causes

Overloading the stomach thereby putting undue pressure on it; exercising after feeding; feeding too soon after strenuous exercise; hereditary defect. A loop forms in the intestine which twists and blocks the digestive tract.

What to do

Seek immediate veterinary attention if bloat is suspected.

Treatment

Fluids are given intravenously to treat for shock, then the air in the stomach is released through a tube which is placed down the trachea into the stomach, or through a canula inserted through the dog's side into the stomach. Surgery is then required to correct the twisted intestine and anchor it in place. Unless this is done swiftly, the dog will die.

Epilepsy

This involves repeated fits or seizures.

Symptoms

Odd, erratic behaviour; screaming for no apparent reason; uncharacteristic aggression; twitching; convulsions (fits); lapses into unconsciousness during which the dog will lie rigid, eyes staring followed by 'jaw-clamping' and 'paddling' with the legs.

Causes

Disturbances in the dog's central nervous system, resulting from electrical abnormalities in the brain. Causes of these include bacterial or viral infections, brain tumours, low levels of calcium in the blood, abnormally low blood-sugar levels, renal (kidney) disease, liver disease and poisoning.

What to do

Don't touch a fitting dog. Take away any objects around him that he could harm himself on. Keep him quiet and, if possible, darken the area. Speak calmly and quietly to comfort and reassure him as he comes out of a fit. Wait until he has fully recovered before taking him to the vet; or ask the vet to come out to him.

Treatment
The cause must be identified before appropriate treatment can be given. Anticonvulsant drugs may be prescribed if fitting is regular and persistent.

Canine infectious hepatitis
This is also known as Rubarth's disease or 'lamp-post disease', because infection is usually through direct or indirect contact with an infected dog's urine, but it is also passed in faeces and saliva.

Symptoms
In a mild form, there is initially depression and loss of appetite with a high temperature, followed by recovery. Some dogs' eyes turn blue a week or so after recovery. In more serious cases, symptoms also include swollen lymph glands, vomiting and diarrhoea (sometimes with blood), plus a painful stomach (due to the enlarged liver). In severe cases, sudden death may be the only indication.

Causes
This is caused by a viral organism called canine adenovirus (CAV-1) that attacks the liver.

What to do
Seek immediate veterinary attention if hepatitis is suspected.

Treatment
Most serious cases die. Mild cases usually recover with supportive veterinary treatment (which may include antibiotics to fight secondary infections, and fluid drips or blood transfusions as necessary), although they remain a danger to others for months after recovery.

Renal failure
This is complete failure of the kidneys.

Symptoms
These include a seemingly insatiable thirst, the passing of large amounts of urine either in one go or at very frequent intervals, vomiting, diarrhoea, loss of appetite, weight loss, halitosis and anaemia.

Causes
For various reasons, including infections and physical damage, the nephrons (parts of the kidneys that remove waste products from the blood) may fail to do their job properly, and this will lead to chronic renal failure. This is an extremely serious and usually irreversible condition with a very poor chance of recovery. The condition rarely occurs in dogs under the age of 5 years.

What to do
Renal failure is life-threatening. Don't hesitate to contact the vet if you suspect this condition in your dog.

Treatment
Treatment of an affected dog may include a period of intensive care, during which the dog will have fluids administered via an intravenous drip, a special diet, coupled with a restful lifestyle and a prescribed course of medication. A dog suffering from renal failure will die, and you may choose to have your pet put to sleep.

Cardiomyopathy
This is disease of the heart muscle.

Symptoms
Any or all of the following: breathlessness, bouts of coughing, extended abdomen, weight loss.

Causes
Usually hereditary or congenital defects, most common in larger breeds of dog.

What to do
Keep the dog calm and don't allow him to exert himself.

Treatment
Occasionally, if detected early enough, surgery may correct the condition.

Poor exercise tolerance
Sometimes a normally active dog will develop problems that make exercise difficult for him.

Symptoms
Pain and discomfort during what should be normal exercise.

Causes
Often a direct result of inflammation of the joints (arthritis), or malformation of the ball-and-socket joints, particularly of the hips. Where a muscle is diseased (for example with a bacterial infection) it is known as myopathy, and where a muscle is inflamed it is known as myositis.

What to do

Make sure your dog is dried off thoroughly if he gets wet – cold and dampness will have a detrimental effect on affected joints. Only administer painkillers on veterinary instruction. Painkillers can easily lull a dog into a false sense of security, causing him to use injured joints which will result in more damage occurring.

Treatment

In cases of mild myopathy, for example where your dog develops a slight limp for 24–36 hours, simply resting him will probably relieve the problem (sometimes it will be necessary to confine him to a limited space, such as a pen). If the limp persists beyond this time, veterinary advice and treatment should be sought; physical and X-ray examinations will be used to confirm diagnosis. When a joint is damaged, the injury is referred to as a sprain, and may involve damage to cartilage and/or ligaments. While not dangerous in itself, the condition is painful. If not treated adequately, a sprain may lead to osteoarthritis. Damage from osteoarthritis is usually permanent.

Obesity

The dog is overweight – even grossly fat, signified by rolls of fat under the skin.

Symptoms

Excess covering of flesh hiding the dog's ribs, which should normally be visible under the skin, particularly as the dog exercises. Breathlessness and a reluctance to exercise; waddling; sluggishness. Obesity can predispose to joint problems and other illnesses

associated with obesity such as heart and major organ failure.

Obesity is very dangerous to a dog of any age: being overweight will shorten a dog's life.

Causes

Old age (not exercising as much), being fed too much food or treats, or being fed an unsuitable diet.

What to do

Consult your vet regarding a suitable diet plan.

Treatment

Exercise your dog more. Follow your vet's diet plan strictly – a change to a specially formulated low-calorie diet will probably be recommended.

Senility

Mental deterioration occurs, usually in old age.

Symptoms

Periods of restlessness, disorientation and abnormal attention-seeking. Incontinence may result.

Causes

Usually due to ageing brain cells no longer being replaced. The disease may also affect the brain and cause premature senility.

What to do

Seek veterinary advice. Give the dog plenty of understanding, love and attention. Ask your vet about special diets formulated for ageing dogs to help delay the onset or slow the process of brain and/or body deterioration.

Treatment

There is no cure, but drug therapy and/or a special diet may help improve quality of life.

Complementary therapies

Increasingly, vets are turning to a more natural approach when treating sick animals, including dogs. Natural medicine involves the use of complementary (natural and traditional) therapies and remedies rather than conventional medicine, which employs synthetic drugs and remedies. A more holistic view is taken of ailments in which the whole animal is considered, rather than simply his condition. Holistic diagnosis takes into account everything on the checklist.

Checklist

✓ overall physical health
✓ mental health
✓ environment
✓ exercise
✓ daily routine
✓ companionship
✓ nutrition (food and water)
✓ hygiene

What is involved?

As soon as the vet or practitioner has ascertained what is ailing the dog, and why, he or she will prescribe the appropriate action or treatment. In some cases, it may simply be a case of improving the dog's environment or exercise levels, or changing the diet to one that better suits his digestive system. In other instances, it may well be that a course of treatment – acupuncture, for example – may have the desired effect in curing whatever is ailing the dog. Sometimes the provision of extra companionship, from either a human or another animal, can alleviate anxiety-induced health problems.

How effective are these therapies?

Many people and vets believe and advocate that these therapies work, and can recount many tales and actual case histories of how natural medicine triumphed where conventional treatment failed. There appears to be little scientific research to substantiate such claims where some therapies are concerned (such as spiritual healing and feng shui), but in truth these remedies have been used for many, even thousands, of years – and something that does not work is unlikely to be persevered with. With most forms of complementary therapy, as long as they are applied with expertise and knowledge, the worst that can happen is that they have no effect on the canine patient. In many instances, they have been proven to bring about apparently miraculous cures.

Aromatherapy, where the dog chooses which oil to sniff, has proved extremely beneficial.

Flower remedies can be administered in drinking water, on a titbit, or via a dropper directly into the mouth.

Top tip

If your dog leads a healthy life in terms of diet, exercise and health care, he is more likely to remain free of ailments.

When to try them

Complementary therapies are so called because most of them are complementary to each other and some can be used simultaneously, or in conjunction with conventional medicine. Better results can be sometimes obtained by using a combination of two or more therapies together to treat a health problem, depending on what the problem is.

Finding a practitioner

More and more vets are using natural healing treatments now, so it is fairly easy to find an experienced and genuine practitioner. Even if your own vet does not personally practise traditional medicine in the particular field you are interested in, he or she may be able to refer you to a reputable person who does. You could also try looking on the internet.

Canine fact

Complementary therapies should not be considered the last resort by pet owners, but as viable forms of treatment that are well worth trying. The range of ailments and conditions that can benefit from natural therapies is vast; a tiny selection of these includes poisoning, diabetes mellitus, osteoarthritis, gingivitis, constipation, cancer, nervousness, aggression, skin diseases, internal and external parasites and anal gland disorders.

Frequently asked question

Q What should I do if my vet won't entertain the idea of any form of 'alternative' treatment but I would like my dog to be treated naturally wherever possible?

A If your vet will not refer you to a complementary practitioner, it may be advisable to take your business to another veterinary clinic that will. You are quite within your rights to do so – after all it is your dog's health that is important, not the feelings of your vet. Ring around veterinary practices in your area – or further afield if you have no other choice – to find one that suits you and your dog's needs. Bear in mind, though, that the further you have to travel, the less convenient it may be in an emergency.

COMPLEMENTARY THERAPIES FOR CANINES

TREATMENT	WHAT IT INVOLVES
Acupressure	Non-invasive pressure is applied to acupoints on the body via the practitioner's fingers or thumb to induce the same reactions in the patient as acupuncture.
Acupuncture	Fine copper or steel special needles are inserted in the skin at specific points (acupoints) on the body to relieve illness and also mental and/or physical stress. This treatment has been shown to alleviate pain, heal damage, promote the body's natural 'feel good' chemicals that produce a sense of well-being, improve appetite and raise energy levels.
Aromatherapy	Essential plant oils – diluted, undiluted or contained in a bland base oil as appropriate – are used to treat ailments. They are applied either by allowing the dog to choose and smell certain oils as its body dictates or by applying them topically where appropriate. They can be used for a whole host of complaints, from flea control to alleviating emotional problems.
Biochemical tissue salts	A form of homoeopathy (see opposite) using 12 energized mineral salts.
Chiropractic	Manipulative method of treating disorders and displacements of joints, especially those in the spine. It can prove useful in cases of back pain, lameness and joint injuries.
Crystals and gems	Through energy waves, each type of crystal can help heal mental and physical ailments. Once the symptoms of the ailment have been determined, the practitioner chooses appropriate stones for the dog to wear, have around his body while resting and/or have in his bed.
Dowsing	Although not a healing treatment in itself, it works as a method of ailment diagnosis by means of a divining rod or a pendulum held over the patient.
Electro-crystal therapy	This enhances the effects of crystals through an energy field created by a small electric charge. Special equipment is used to effect this painless treatment.
Feng shui	This ancient Chinese art involves arranging your dog's home environment to optimize his mental and physical well-being. Acupuncture was derived from this practice.
Flower remedies	These are essences derived from specific flower petals which are floated in water to transfer their healing properties into the liquid, to which a tiny amount of alcohol (usually brandy) is added to preserve them. Essences are available for all sorts of behavioural problems, including anxiety, aggression, timidity and shock. They appear also to alleviate physical ailments, if these are linked to mental or emotional problems.

COMPLEMENTARY THERAPIES FOR CANINES

TREATMENT	WHAT IT INVOLVES
Herbalism	Plant-based natural medicines for both external and internal use. For example, the willow tree is a source of salicylic acid (aspirin), while digitalis (heart medicine) is derived from foxglove. An infusion of mallow can be used to bathe swollen areas to reduce swelling, while comfrey can be taken internally to help repair bone fractures.
Homoeopathy	Remedies derived from animal, mineral and vegetable substances through a special process called 'potentization' that releases their therapeutic properties. It works on the principle of 'like cures like': if a substance causes adverse symptoms in an animal, a minute 'energized' dose of it can also cure those same symptoms. Remedies include those from seemingly strange sources such as lead, poisonous snake venom, arsenic, egg yolk and animal tissue among many others.
Iridology	Ailments are diagnosed by examining the iris of the eye; minute changes in its colour and shape can inform the practitioner about the patient's health status, the location and type of disease present in the body, and whether the dog will have a tendency towards disease in the future.
Kinesiology	Testing muscles that relate to an organ system through an energy field (the dog) to determine imbalances.
Magnotherapy	The use of magnets to promote healing, through increasing blood supply to the afflicted area.
Osteopathy	Manipulative adjustment of muscles and joints to relieve misalignment that is causing pain.
Physiotherapy	Involves body manipulation, massage, exercise, specialized machines (such as ultrasound) and the application of warmth or cold as appropriate to help treat disease, injury or deformity.
Radionics	This distance healing works via the practitioner assessing a 'witness' (a lock of hair, for example) from the patient to determine what ails him, then directing healing energy vibrations at him through a specialized radionics instrument known as the 'black box'.
Reflexology	Diseases of body organs are treated by applying pressure to particular joints.
Spiritual (faith) healing	The 'laying-on of hands' on the animal or his affected area: healing powers are directed at the patient via a medium through the actual healer. This form of healing has proven effective with 'incurable' diseases such as cancer, though is not guaranteed to work – it depends on the individual dog.
Touch massage	Gentle, repetitive massaging movements, which are said to generate specific brainwave patterns in the recipient that help promote mental and physical healing.

Caring for the older (senior) dog

An ageing dog, if he is in good health, can provide companionship that is just as rewarding as playing with a puppy. The old dog's reactions may not be as sharp, nor may he move as fast or be as agile when playing 'fetch' with you, but you and he will gain as much pleasure from your relationship as you did when he was younger. He may sit around a lot and be undemanding and quiet, but an elderly dog should not be ignored. To remain contented and in the best possible health, he needs everything on the checklist.

Checklist

✓ lots of love and affection
✓ keeping warm
✓ particular attention to teeth and possibly nails
✓ extra care with diet
✓ exercise dependent on his physical condition
✓ help with grooming
✓ twice-yearly veterinary check-ups
✓ patience and understanding if toileting accidents occur
✓ constant daily routine
✓ minimal upheaval
✓ plenty of sleep

If your elderly dog displays an increased need for your company, give him plenty of attention and reassurance – even consider moving his bed into your bedroom at night if necessary. Leaving a radio on low while you are out can help provide 'company' through the sound of voices while you are out.

Being less active as they grow older, it is easy for elderly dogs to pile on weight, which can put undue strain on the heart and joints, so a careful watch must be kept on this. Equally, they can lose weight rapidly and starve if they are not eating for any reason.

Signs of ageing

Signs of old age in a dog are not difficult to spot: he starts to take things easy, spends more time than usual sleeping, and his ease of movement reduces; some dogs suffer failing eyesight and/or hearing. In black-coated individuals, grey areas around the muzzle develop and sometimes close to the eyes, although the overall body colour is unaffected.

Lifestyle

Everything should be done to keep the elderly dog feeling as good as possible. Disturbed behaviour patterns may be the result of chronic physical or mental illness (brain degeneration – the canine equivalent of Alzheimer's disease in humans) in the old dog. For example, a previously clean dog may have accidents, making 'piles and puddles' on the floor or even furniture. If this happens, it may be best to keep your pet in areas of the house where such accidents don't matter – but that does not mean he should be shut away or limited in his access to his family, as this would be unfair and cruel. It would also be unfair and cruel to chastise or ban the dog from the house for something that is beyond his control.

If your dog has remained fit and active throughout his life, carry on exercising him as normal on the basis that 'if he doesn't use it, he will lose it'. He will tell you when he needs to slow down, and providing you are alert to your dog's needs you will know when and how much to ease off.

If his eyesight and hearing begin to fail, he can still enjoy life, but you may have to adapt your command signals to him so he can understand what you want. Clapping can help a blind dog, while visual signals (by hand or flashlight) can direct a deaf dog.

For holiday care, see pages 102–103.

Canine fact

Just like elderly people, old dogs are resistant to and can be upset by major changes in their routine and lifestyle. If changes do have to happen, try to incorporate them gradually to allow your dog time to get used to them.

Diet

Foods specially formulated for senior dogs are available, and these contain all the nutrients the ageing body needs to remain in the best possible condition and help delay or alleviate the onset of conditions such as senility. As older dogs can often suffer from liver-failure problems, a low-protein diet may be applicable; consult your vet regarding the best type of food for your dog. Older dogs may not be as able to defend their food as they once could, so if you have other dogs make quite sure they are not allowed to steal his meals, or intimidate him while he is eating and scare him off.

If his eyesight (and/or hearing) is failing, get your older dog used to certain walks so that his other senses take over and he feels secure and happy on these. Keep everything in the same position in the house so that a visually impaired dog can 'mind-map' them and negotiate his way around without fear of bumping into things and injuring himself.

Frequently asked question

Q How do canine and human ages compare?

A This depends on the breed of dog, as some have much shorter life expectancies than others; as an approximate guide only, equate 14 human years to the first year of a dog's life and add 7 for each following year.

AGE OF DOG	EQUIVALENT AGE OF HUMAN
1	14
2	21
3	28
4	35
5	42
6	49
7	56
8	63
9	70
10	77
11	84
12	91

With advances in veterinary medicine and life-stage dog foods, many dogs are able to live a longer and fuller life. As a general rule, smaller dogs live longer than larger ones. For example Irish Wolfhounds only live for 8–9 years, whereas a Yorkshire Terrier may still be going strong at 15.

Common ailments

As a dog ages, so a certain amount of body tissue degeneration occurs. This is inevitable and cannot be prevented, although with owner and veterinary care the

Did you know ...?

A frequently seen problem in old dogs is known as 'geriatric separation anxiety', signs of which become apparent at night when the rest of the household is asleep. The dog wakes up and feels disorientated. He starts barking and panting, showing signs of obvious anxiety; in an extreme case he may even soil his surroundings. It is comparable to a severe panic attack in humans. If there is no underlying cause for this distressing behaviour, such as a tumour, then drugs (and in some cases, alternative remedies) can be given to treat your pet's anxiety and so help resolve the problem. Interestingly, dogs who were nervous when younger appear to be most vulnerable to this condition.

effects can be eased. Once your dog reaches the age of 7 (or 5 if it is a giant breed) you should take him for twice-yearly check-ups with your vet, so that any problems can be diagnosed and treated at an early stage. Old dogs are prone to certain ailments that include:

- liver disease
- joint stiffness and arthritis
- coat and skin complaints
- constipation due to decreased digestive efficiency
- tooth and gum problems
- injury due to decrease in agility
- cold-related problems due to decreased body temperature regulation
- incontinence
- deafness
- senility
- hearing and sight problems
- obesity-related problems
- loss of appetite
- heart disease

Seek veterinary advice for all of these ailments – the quicker they are dealt with, the more likely the outcome will be successful in prolonging your pet's life comfortably.

Companionship

Some people consider getting a puppy when their established dog gets old. This can be a good or bad decision depending on the temperament and nature of the aged dog;

Top tip

The key to good health care for your old dog lies in vigilance. Twice-yearly check-ups by a vet will alert them to early signs of problems; some vets run clinics for older dogs, recognizing the need to spend a little extra time on these much-cherished companions. Extra attention should be given to grooming the old dog, as he may find self-grooming difficult if he is stiff or suffers from arthritis – especially in hard-to-reach places, such as under his tail; nails may need regular trimming if they are not kept worn down through exercise outside.

Bad or worn teeth and inflamed gums are not uncommon in old canines; at this stage, your dog will find soft moist or semi-moist food easier to eat. Give him chews and bones (see pages 38–45) to gnaw on to help keep his teeth in as good a condition as possible.

if he likes the puppy, then he may gain a new lease of life. If, however, he doesn't, or cannot cope with the puppy's liveliness and mischievousness, he may resent the newcomer and become depressed and withdrawn, stop eating and, ultimately, become very ill. If the old dog is the only one in the household and has always been a loner, then it would be kinder not to get another dog or puppy.

Another consideration is that as the puppy matures it is likely to exert dominance challenges over the older, weaker dog, which will make the latter's life miserable.

Time to say goodbye

Eventually the older dog sleeps more and more and is increasingly reluctant to exercise. While he is able to function normally, if only in this modified way, he is probably quite happy and contented. If his bladder, bowels and limbs begin to fail and he is unable to function without mental distress or physical pain, you must seek veterinary advice, for the only humane thing to do in these circumstances is to have the old dog euthanized, allowing him to die painlessly and with dignity. (See pages 186–189 for information on bereavement and euthanasia.)

Bereavement

If a much-loved pet dies, or his death is imminent, it often has a deep impact on those humans who loved and cared for him. For many owners, losing a cherished companion is similar to coping with the death of a family member or close friend. Different people deal with this trauma in different ways, but all or some of the stages of grief that are often encountered are shown on the checklist.

Checklist

- ✓ anticipation of loss
- ✓ shock
- ✓ denial
- ✓ anger
- ✓ depression
- ✓ acceptance

Why pet dogs die

A dog may die for one of two reasons:

1 sudden death through accident or illness.
2 euthanasia (being 'put to sleep' or 'put down') following an accident or due to illness, when a cure is not possible and the dog's quality of life is or will be poor.

If sudden, you will not be prepared for your dog's death and it will no doubt come as a huge shock. If he has to be put down, you can prepare for the inevitable, although it does not make it any easier to bear. Many owners blame themselves for their pet's death, and agonize over whether the death could have been prevented if they had done things differently. This is a normal reaction, but sadly it cannot change what has happened. Try to focus on the many happy times you enjoyed with your cherished pet and to treasure those memories.

Euthanasia

Other than sudden death, having a dog put down is the most humane way for him to die. A prolonged natural death can be traumatic for both pet and owner, as well as painful for the former. While the process may be upsetting to read about, it can help to understand how euthanasia is achieved. Talk it over with your vet first and decide whether having it done at home or at the vet clinic would be most suitable and practical. Also discuss the options of what to do with your pet's body. Once this has been mutually agreed, then arrange a date – preferably sooner rather than later so as

not to prolong your dog's suffering, as well as your own, unnecessarily.

At the veterinary clinic

Arrange a time when the vet clinic is likely to be quiet, or you can enter and leave through a private entrance so that you do not have to face a crowded waiting room. Have a supportive person drive you there and back; you may well be upset, and therefore in no fit state to undertake this yourself. Take a blanket in which to wrap your pet to bring him home again if this is what you want to do.

Did you know ...?

Being animal-lovers themselves, many vets find euthanizing pets as painful as the owners (especially if the pet is well known to them), although it does not stop them being professional about it. Just because a vet may appear to be detached about the process does not mean that he or she does not care; they do, it is just they have to remain strong for the animals' – and often the owners' – sake. Many vets are now more aware of the fact that owners suffer great emotional pain when they lose a pet, and are better equipped to cope with this than they may have been years ago; and because of this they offer a much more sympathetic and caring service.

Make the journey there as smooth, stress-free and quiet as possible. If you will be able to bear up in your dog's last moments, then be with him. If you feel you will go to pieces, then ask your vet and the vet nurse to deal with it; if you are terribly distressed, it may make your pet equally so and his passing may not be as peaceful as it should be.

At home

This is more expensive, but may be the preferred option if you are unable to get to the clinic, your dog is too ill to move, he finds travel upsetting, or you would prefer euthanasia to be done in familiar and comfortable surroundings. Request that a vet nurse attends, as well as the vet. The former can help out as required or where necessary, and help to keep you and the dog calm, thereby making the process as stress-free as possible.

On the day, keep your dog's routine beforehand as normal, but give him lots of extra attention and cuddles – he may not understand why you are being extra-affectionate, but may appreciate it nonetheless, and at least it will make you feel better as well as make the most of those last precious moments.

The process

Properly carried out, the process is quick and relatively painless. A sedative injection may be given if the dog is very distressed or is difficult to handle or restrain. A foreleg is usually shaved to identify where the relevant vein is situated. An injection comprising an overdose of anaesthetic is given in this vein; this causes the dog to become drowsy, lapse into unconsciousness and die peacefully in seconds. If the necessary leg vein is not easy to find, the vet may need to inject directly into the heart or kidneys. Owners can find

Canine fact

Sometimes owners cannot bear to lose their pet – which is understandable – and delay having him put down when really it should be done sooner rather than later. However, a caring owner will put their pet's needs first, not their own – no matter the cost to themselves.

However hard it may be to face up to the loss, having him euthanized is the kindest thing you can do for a dog that is suffering, to save him from further distress.

this distressing, so this is where the experienced handling and sympathetic soothing of the dog afforded by a vet nurse can prove beneficial to all concerned.

Afterwards

Either the vet will dispose of the body, arrange to have it buried or cremated on your instructions, or you can take it home, if this is allowable, to bury in a favoured area of the garden. Graves should be at least 1m (3ft 3in) deep and well away from water courses (your local environment agency should be able to advise you). Pet cemeteries and crematoriums will advise you on cost and what is involved.

Grief

It is important to realize that grieving is an essential part of the healing process after bereavement. There is no set time limit as to how long owners should grieve: some are able to accept and recover from the loss more easily than others, who may not get over it for months, even years. However long it takes, do not be afraid to grieve when you feel the need to; bottling up grief inside you is bound to affect your own mental and physical health.

Help when you need it most

Sometimes you may feel as though you are over the loss, but then grief hits you again at unexpected moments – such as

Top tip

Physically marking your dog's passing with a grave and monument to show where he lies – such as a headstone, tree, shrub or plants – can prove therapeutic in that you have somewhere tangible to go to mourn your pet, and remember him with gladness when the raw grief subsides. Alternatively, you could make a donation – either a one-off or annually on your dog's birthday or day of passing – to an animal rescue centre to mark his life. You can also put obituaries in dog magazines and post them on websites specially designed for this purpose – simply key in 'pet loss' to a search engine and you will find a number of sites.

when something triggers memories of your dog – and feelings of extreme sadness engulf you all over again. Don't be afraid to lean on supportive family and friends when you feel the need, and do make use of the many excellent pet-bereavement counselling services that are available by phone, letter and email – many animal charities provide such a service, as do some pet insurance companies. If overwhelming sorrow persists longer than you feel able to cope with, go and see an understanding doctor; it may be that you need additional counselling, or even prescribed medication, to help ease debilitating grief and allow you to function with some normality again.

Children and pet loss

Depending on their age, children react differently to the death of a pet – and for many it will the first time they experience this inevitable part of life. This being the case, it will help enormously for a parent to talk things through with a bereavement counsellor as to how to approach and explain pet death. The child too may find such supportive third-party help invaluable.

Never underestimate a child's grief or reaction to the death of a pet, as it can affect them in many different ways that can have long-lasting and detrimental effects on their behaviour, health, learning ability and socialization. One thing that is advisable not to do is to say that the pet was 'put to sleep' as this can create false hope; the child may think that one day their doggy friend will wake up and come back again.

Whether a child should be allowed to see the body of the pet depends on the age and psyche of the child, and a qualified counsellor will be able to advise on the best course of action to take.

Pet grief

It is not just the owner that grieves over the loss of a pet; so can other animals in the household. Some people prefer to let the other animals see the body of their friend so they recognize it has died and say 'goodbye'. The best thing to do is to carry on with the remaining pets' routine as normal, and to let them work out a new hierarchy among themselves. Perhaps the last thing you need right now are the potential problems that introducing a new pet into the equation may well bring.

When you feel the time is right to get another dog, remember that there are plenty of homeless dogs waiting in rescue centres for good homes.

Frequently asked question

Q I'm getting on in years and am worried what will happen to my dog if I die before he does. How can I make sure that he will be well cared for when I am gone?

A This is a very real worry for caring senior owners who may not be in the best of health, or know they are quite likely to die before their pet does. If no relatives are willing to give the dog a good permanent home, then some animal charities will take on this responsibility and find the dog a home his old owner would have approved of. To ensure that this happens in event of death, the owner (or his/her representative) should contact a charity that makes such provisions to find out what they need to do beforehand, so that when the time comes the dog can be transferred to the charity or new home with the minimum of fuss and stress.

Top tip

After the death of a dog, don't get another one just on the basis that you think it will be beneficial to surviving pet(s) (although in some cases this has proved a success) as they may resent an 'intruder'. If you want to get another dog, wait until you feel emotionally and physically ready to cope with a new addition to the household.

INDEX

ACKNOWLEDGEMENTS

Executive Editor Trevor Davies
Managing Editor Clare Churly
Executive Art Editor Leigh Jones
Designer Jo Tapper
Picture Library Assistant Luzia Strohmayer
Senior Production Controller Manjit Sihra

Photographic Acknowledgements in Source Order

Ardea/John Daniels 5 top right, 8 left, 8 bottom right, 12, 24, 128 bottom, 148, 149, 151, 184
Bruce Coleman Collection/Jane Burton 129 top left, 152
Corbis UK Ltd/George Lepp 142 centre/**Touhig Sion** 177/**Jean-Bernard Vernier** 51 top
Frank Lane Picture Agency/Foto Natura 18 bottom right, 77 bottom, 187/**Gerard Lacz** 58 bottom right, 62 bottom left/**Minden Pictures** 51 bottom/**Martin B Withers** 169
Family Life Picture Library/Angela Hampton 29, 142 top, 170 bottom, 172
Getty Images/Deborah Gilbert 38
NHPA/Susanne Danegger 9 bottom left, 49 /**E A Janes** 84 bottom right, 97 bottom

Octopus Publishing Group Limited 32 top, 66, 101 bottom, 167/**Jane Burton** 1, 2-3, 154, 155, 156, 157/**Stephen Conroy** 44/**Steve Gorton** 50, 54, 55, 58 top right, 59 top left, 59 top right, 60 bottom right, 60 bottom left, 61 top centre, 61 top left, 61 top right, 61 bottom right, 61 bottom left, 62 top, 62 bottom right, 63 top left, 63 top right, 63 bottom, 65, 67, 70, 71 bottom, 82 top, 82 bottom, 89 top, 91 bottom, 124, 129 top right, 137, 139, 145, 185/**Rosie Hyde** 4, 5 bottom right, 5 bottom left, 7 top right, 7 bottom right, 7 bottom left, 9 top right, 23, 28, 36 bottom, 43 top, 57, 62 centre left, 62 centre right, 68, 84 top right, 85 top left, 85 top right, 85 bottom left, 90, 92, 94, 95, 97 top, 100 left, 100 right, 101 top left, 101 top right, 104 left, 104 top right, 107, 110 left, 112, 113 bottom, 138, 147, 153, 162/**Rosie Hyde/Stonehenge Veterinary Hospital** 168 top,171 /**Ray Moller** 14 top, 15, 17, 18, 46/**Angus Murray** 5 centre right, 6, 7 top left, 8 top right, 9 top left, 10, 14 centre, 14 bottom, 21, 30, 31, 32 bottom, 33 top, 34, 35, 37, 39, 42, 45, 47, 48 top right, 48 bottom right, 59 bottom left, 60 top left, 60 top right, 62 centre, 71 top, 72, 73, 74, 75, 81, 84 left, 85 bottom right, 86, 87 left, 87 right, 87 centre, 88, 89 bottom, 91 top, 96, 104 bottom right, 105 top left, 105 top right, 105 bottom right, 105 bottom left, 108, 109,

110 right, 111 left, 111 right, 113 top, 114, 114 right, 115, 116 left, 116 right, 116 centre, 117 left, 117 right, 118 left, 118 right, 118 centre, 119 top left, 119 top right, 119 bottom right, 119 bottom left, 120 left, 120 right, 120 centre, 121 top left, 121 top right, 121 bottom right, 121 bottom left, 122 top, 122 centre, 122 bottom, 123 top, 123 bottom right, 123 bottom left, 123 bottom centre, 125 left, 125 right, 126 top, 126 bottom right, 126 bottom left, 127 top left, 127 top right, 127 bottom right, 127 bottom left, 127 bottom centre /**Tim Ridley** 5, 11, 22, 26, 33 bottom, 48 left, 52, 53, 58, 76, 77 top, 80, 83, 103, 106, 182, 189 /**L Wickenden** 36 top, 40 top, 40 centre, 40 bottom
RSPCA Photolibrary/David Dalton 9 bottom right, 27/**Cheryl A Ertelt** 159, 164/**Angela Hampton** 141/**Robert Jones** 170 top/**Nikita Ovsyanikov** 64/**Tim Sambrook** 102/**Colin Seddon** 144
Shoot Photographic/John Daniels 43 bottom, 69, 128 top, 140, 142 bottom, 183
Solitaire Photographic/Angela Rixon 129 bottom right, 129 bottom left, 165, 173
Warren Photographic/Jane Burton 13, 93, 158, 160 top, 160 centre left, 160 bottom left, 161, 168 bottom, 174, 178
Your Dog Magazine 179